How to Get Started
IN
Real Estate
Investing

Other McGraw-Hill Books by Robert Irwin

How to Get Started
in
Real Estate
Investing

Second Edition

ROBERT IRWIN

Mc
Graw
Hill

New York   Chicago   San Francisco   Lisbon   London
Madrid   Mexico City   Milan   New Delhi   San Juan
Seoul   Singapore   Sydney   Toronto

1 2 3 4 5 6 7 8 9 0   FGR/FGR   0 9 8

ISBN 978-0-07-183285-4

MHID: 0-07-150836-8

This publication is designed to provide accurate and authoritative information in regard to the subject matter covered. It is sold with the understanding that the publisher and the author are not engaged in rendering legal, accounting, or other professional service. If legal advice or other expert assistance is required, the services of a competent professional person should be sought.

—From a declaration of principles jointly adopted by a committee
of the American Bar Association and a committee of publishers.

McGraw-Hill books are available at special quantity discounts to use as premiums and sales promotions, or for use in corporate training programs. To contact a representative please visit the Contact Us pages at www.mhprofessional.com.

REALTOR® is a registered collective membership mark which may be used only by real estate professionals who are members of the NATIONAL ASSOCIATION OF REALTORS ® and subscribe to its strict Code of Ethics.

Contents

Preface

When I wrote the first edition of this book back in 2002, we were just starting the biggest real estate boom in the history of this country. Prices were shooting up, and properties were selling like hotcakes.

Today, as we all know, things are quite different.

Yet, in many ways, today's market offers an even better time to get started in real estate investing. Today, there are more bargains, if you know where to look. Today, the threshold for getting in has been lowered, so almost anyone can get started. And today, there are fewer competitors.

In fact, I can't remember a more opportune time to get started in real estate investing. This is one reason why I wrote this new second edition—to show readers like you how to get started in a challenging market.

The second reason is that I wanted to answer a criticism of the first book.

The first edition of this book started with a narrative chapter, something that was quite out of the ordinary for a business or real estate tome. It followed an industrious couple from the purchase of their first home through moving up to rental properties.

I guess lots of people liked it because the book sold hundreds of thousands of copies. However, any time you write a lot of books

(I've written well over 50), you come in for your share of criticism as well. Some of the complaints I heard about the first edition were, "It ends too soon" and "It doesn't show more complex investments."

In the second edition, therefore, I'm going to try to take this book a step further. This edition still shows all about getting started with your first investment house. It still starts off with a narrative chapter in which beginning investors buy a home.* However, in this edition, our new characters go much further: into foreclosures, Section 1031 tax-deferred exchanges, and commercial real estate. My second goal is to make these more sophisticated areas as understandable and accessible as the first edition made the buying of homes.

If you're wondering about getting started in real estate investing, you'll find this book a wonderful place to begin—its step-by-step approach simplifies and encourages. If you're already an investor, you'll find answers to your questions as you progress to more sophisticated properties.

People are still making their fortunes in real estate. Don't you be the one to miss out.

---

*The characters mentioned in the examples in this book are fictional, and any resemblance to real people living or dead is coincidental.

How to Get Started

IN

Real Estate Investing

How to Get Started Investing in Real Estate

There's a common tendency to look at successful real estate investors and wish you were like them. Perhaps you know several such people. It could be a neighbor who owns a half-dozen homes and rents them out. Or perhaps it's a relative who's done well and now commands the rents from an apartment building. Or perhaps your real estate idols run to the well known, such as Donald Trump or Conrad Hilton.

Of course, the really big question is, how do you get there? If you're propertyless (and perhaps don't have a lot of cash), is there any hope for you? Maybe you own your home and you now want to move up to a rental. Or you may even be a more involved investor who owns several properties, and now you want to move from residential to commercial developments.

The question for you in all these cases is the same: How? How do you get from where you are to the level of successful real estate investors?

Quite frankly, this is a question that most books on real estate investing try to answer. They often do it with a series of inspirational chapters interwoven with some basic instruction, all held together by the author's personal experiences. This can be entertaining, but it's typically not the kind of how-to instruction that I suspect most people who want to move up in real estate really crave.

Therefore, to help you get from here to there, this first chapter follows an average couple as they struggle to get started. We'll see them purchase their first property. (It happens to be a foreclosure.) They'll do a trade, and even progress to commercial property, as they begin to amass their fortune.

I'll try to make the process as clear as possible. You'll see the steps they take, their mistakes, and their successes. Of course, the characters described are fictional; they are drawn from many real estate investors I've known over the years. However, the situations they are in and the profits they make are indicative of what real people in the field are doing all the time.

Of course, since we're starting at the beginning, if you're already an experienced investor, you might prefer to proceed directly to the later chapters of this book. However, I suspect that at some point, you'll want to return to this chapter, if for no other reason than to review the basics of getting started investing in real estate. You may be surprised to find information here that you thought you knew, but in fact weren't quite up to speed on.

It's All about Making Choices

Bob (not yours truly) and Jane had been married for nearly 5 years. They had a small family (one child), they both worked hard, and they lived in a nice apartment. However, one thing had become abundantly clear to them: they would never really rise, economically speaking, by continuing to do what they were doing.

Their goal was to retire early. But like most people, they were really just making ends meet—just getting by.

They did have some savings and some investments. However, they had lost much of their investment capital in stock market crashes, and Bob, in particular, was averse to venturing more into stocks. He felt that what they had should just be in CDs, where it could "safely" earn interest. (I put the quotes around "safely" because inflation and taxation tended to erode their capital.)

Real estate held Jane and Bob's interest, especially during the "bubble" in the early part of the decade. They watched with envy as prices skyrocketed and the "people next door" were apparently turned into instant millionaires. But it always seemed that a piece of property was just a little bit out of their reach, just too expensive for them.

Then, almost overnight, the real estate bubble burst. It was as if one day nothing was for sale, and the next day, everything was. Prices fell. Builders offered auctions. Foreclosures were rampant. And those "instant millionaires" were suddenly facing bankruptcy.

"How could this have happened?" Bob wondered. He said, "I'm really glad we never bought property." But Jane wasn't so sure. "Maybe with the market down, now would be the perfect time to jump in. We certainly could afford to buy something now, couldn't we?"

Bob wasn't sure. Then they had a meeting with their accountant, who told them that they needed to shelter some of their income. He said that they were "wasting" money in taxes because they were renters. None of the money that they paid in rent was tax-deductible. On the other hand, if they bought a house, the interest and taxes would be deductible (up to certain limits; see Chapter 13.) "Buy a home," he said. "It's a no-brainer."

Jane pointed out that in addition to tax savings, a house would also give them more privacy, more space and, in general, more control over their environment.

But Bob still wasn't sure. The real estate market in their area had tanked. Prices had moved down. Inventories were still high. And nothing was selling. Jane pointed out, "I think that's called a 'buyer's market'—and we're buyers."

So they opened the local newspaper and were faced with dozens and dozens of "For Sale" advertisements. The prices were all over the charts. There were single-family homes and condos. Some had pools, some had big lots, and some even had room for horses. And those were just the resales. There was also a host of brand new homes for sale, with builders offering "incentives" to buy and move in.

"We obviously can find a house we would like to live in, but will it be a good investment as well?" Bob asked. Jane shook her head. She had no idea. So they decided to contact an expert, someone who specialized in real estate. They decided to meet with an agent.

They didn't know any agents, but one of Jane's friends had recently bought a home and had raved about Leo, the Realtor® she used. So, on her recommendation, they went to see Leo. (A Realtor is a member of the National Association of Realtors [NAR®], a trade group dedicated to promoting better business practices; an agent is a generic term denoting a person who is licensed to sell real estate.)

The office Leo was working in was quite active, with lots of agents scurrying around. However, when they asked for Leo, they were escorted to a quiet little corner room in the back. Leo appeared to be in his sixties. He introduced himself, had them sit down, and then began talking about his life. He said he had been in real estate for over 35 years.

He had worked as a butcher and a salesman for butcher knives. But he had decided that he wanted to get ahead financially, so he moved into real estate.

Besides being a Realtor, Leo owned lots of rentals—houses, apartments, and commercial buildings. But he still worked full-time in an active office. He said it helped him, "Keep on top of things." He said that he had sold five properties in the last six months and that he would be happy to give them a list of his previous customers. He encouraged them to call those customers to see how others had fared with him. Jane took the list and carefully put it in her purse. (She made the calls later.)

Then Bob explained their situation. He said they had a little money saved. They had good, but not great credit. And they wanted to buy a home both as an investment and to shelter some of their income. Their big question was, "What makes a good starter investment property?"

Leo nodded to indicate that he understood their situation. He sat back and explained that he had three general rules that he followed and that always had done well by him in real estate.

Flippable/Holdable/Profitable

1. **"You must buy low."** "Think of it this way," Leo said. "You make your profit when you buy, not when you sell. If you buy low enough, then you will be able to either rent out the property for a positive cash flow and hold it for a long-term profit over time or sell it quickly (flip it) for a quick profit."

2. **"You improve your profit by improving your property."** "One way to get a property at a low cost is to buy a fixer-upper (one that's in run-down condition, sometimes called a 'handyman's special'). Such a property can often be bought for far below market price. Fixing it up brings up its value—and your profit."

3. **"You play the market: depending on the property and market conditions, you either 'buy and hold' or 'buy and flip.'"** "In a down market where buyers are scarce, if you buy right, you can rent out the property indefinitely. As your tenants slowly pay down your mortgage, and as inflation boosts the property's value, your equity will rise. Eventually you can either resell for a profit or refinance to take

money out. In a hot market, or when you get a 'steal,' you can flip the property for a quick profit."

"Of course, there are other rules to follow," Leo added. "But, if you let these three basic ones guide you, you won't go far wrong."

The Starter

"Okay," Bob said. "That's all well and good for general principles. But where do we start? When we looked in the paper, we saw houses, condos, co-ops, and small apartment buildings. Do we just throw a dart?"

"Without question," Leo replied, "the first thing you should buy is a home in which to live. It's everyone's first step."

This time Jane was puzzled. "You said we should get an investment. But now you're saying we should buy a residence. I don't get it. Aren't we going in two different directions?"

"Not at all," Leo said. "Your first home will also be your first investment property. If you buy wisely, it will initially be your residence. Later, you can convert it to a rental, an investment."

Bob shook his head. "It doesn't make sense. Why not buy a rental to begin with?"

"The answer to that," Leo said, "has to do with how real estate is financed."

Starter Financing

Leo explained that because of its high price, relatively little real estate is purchased for cash. "It's not like most stocks and bonds, which the investor buys outright. In real estate, most people, most investors, get financing. They get OPM, which is an acronym that stands for 'other people's money.' In this case we're talking about getting money from a financial institution such as a bank, an insurance company, or even a private individual. The lender puts up most of the money so that you can purchase the property."

The trick is to understand that the very best financing in the world (low or nothing down, a lower interest rate, lower payments) is available for the purchase of a home in which you intend to live.

Both Jane and Bob still looked a little puzzled, so Leo went on. He explained that to buy a commercial piece of property, such as an office building, shopping mall, or industrial park, the lender would require the buyer to put up at least 20 to 25 percent or more of the purchase price in cash. (If the property cost a million dollars, that would be at least $200,000 to $250,000.)

"But when you buy a home *in which you plan to live*, whether it be a single-family detached house, a condo, or up to a four-unit apartment house (in which you would live in one unit), the down payment is reduced, and often so are the interest rate and the monthly payment.

"On a home/residence you could put as little as 10 percent down. Indeed, until the credit crunch of 2007, 100 percent financing—nothing down—was readily available. And even that's coming back again."

"Let me get this straight," Bob said. "If we buy a home in which we plan to live, we get this great financing. But if we buy a home or other property that we plan to rent out or resell, we don't."

"That's it in a nutshell," Leo said. (See also Chapter 10 for a further explanation of why.)

"Then later," Jane continued, "after we've lived there for a while, we can convert it to a rental? And that's okay?"

"Yes," Leo said. "Once you're in your property and have lived in it for a while, you can do what you want with it. You're entitled to sell it—or, normally, to rent it out."

"But," Jane pressed on, "if we rent it out, where will we live?"

"Why," said Leo, "you simply buy another house and move on. There are many people who never get farther in real estate than this. They are called 'serial home investors,' and some of them have dozens and dozens of homes. They often live off their rental income and refinance or sell only when they need money or find another, better investment opportunity. Many of these successful investors take six-month vacations and have multiple residences in different parts of the country. I myself, for example, have a personal residence here in town, and another at Lake Tahoe in the mountains."

"So all we'll do is buy homes and convert them to rentals, right?" said Bob.

"No," replied Leo, "not at all. While you can do only that if you choose, there's a world of other opportunities, such as office buildings, land development, motels/hotels, industrial buildings, strip malls (or larger), and on and on. But the only way to really get your feet wet is to buy your first home to live in."

Dual Criteria

"Let's do it," Jane said. Bob nodded in agreement: "It sounds like something that would work for us."

"Okay," said Leo. "But before you begin, let's define some criteria. Remember, you're not just looking for a home in which to live—one that you personally like. You're also looking for a home that you can later resell for a profit and/or rent. The house has to meet two *sets of criteria—personal use and later investment use.*"

Leo said that he used the "four-out-of-five rule." If four out of five buyers will like something about a home, that feature will help resell it in the future, even if you personally dislike the feature. "If only one out of five will like it (especially if that one is you), it's going to hold *back* the home's resale.

"Take paint color as an example," Leo said. "You may not particularly care for light, bland colors. But most buyers don't object to them. Therefore a light-colored home typically will sell faster and for more money than a home colored in vivid blues or dark browns."

TIP

For an investment, plan your resale (or your rental) when you buy. Look for what most buyers (or tenants) will want. When buying for profit, you should think less about what you would ideally want in a house and much more about what the next buyers (or a tenant) would want.

Leo went on to explain the set of resale criteria—what makes a house desirable to the next set of buyers.

The "Next-Buyer" Criteria

Good Neighborhood Schools

Leo pointed out that nothing made a home more valuable as an investment than having good neighborhood schools. Studies have repeatedly showed that the better the schools, the faster and higher home prices appreciated. Indeed, in areas where schools were poor, home prices sometimes went the other way, down!

TIP

You can find out about the quality of the nearby schools by simply giving the local school district a call. All districts have standardized test scores that are available to the public. Also, many Web sites offer these statistics.

Pride of Ownership Evident in the Neighborhood

This time Jane was puzzled. She said she certainly had heard of pride of ownership, but she found it hard to understand. Leo said it was easier to see than to describe. When all the homes in a neighborhood are well painted and well landscaped, and there is no trash out front (or cars being worked on), it indicates that the neighbors are proud of their homes. Buying a home in this kind of well-kept neighborhood would pay good dividends later on (would make a wise investment) when Jane and Bob resold it. Jane nodded. Bob seemed unconvinced. He liked to work on his car in the driveway.

Low Crime Rate in the Neighborhood

Leo pointed out that Bob and Jane naturally didn't want to live in a high-crime area. But they probably hadn't given it much thought. Leo now emphasized how important it was. He pointed out that while no area is completely safe, many areas have significantly lower crime rates than others. People with families as well as singles and couples prefer the low-crime areas. Jane nodded in agreement here. Again, Bob didn't seem to think it was that important.

Leo then said that this was also a parameter for a rental. He asked, "How would you like to try to collect rents in a high-crime area? Planning ahead, you may someday want to rent out the house you're now buying. Someone might be out there ready to steal your hard-earned rents from you before you got home." Bob admitted that when Leo put it that way, it made a lot of sense.

Leo said he had his own way of telling how crime-ridden a neighborhood is. He called it his "graffiti index." The more graffiti on the walls and fences, the worse the crime rate in the area. On the other hand, if neighbors quickly paint over graffiti or if graffiti seldom appear, there is generally less crime and less gang activity.

T I P

You can learn about the crime rate in a neighborhood by calling the public affairs office of the local police department, which often provides crime statistics not only by neighborhood but by street and block as well.

Close to Shopping and with Access to Transportation

Leo pointed out that these days, when traffic congestion is a major concern in virtually all cities, having access to freeways, buses, trains, and other forms of transportation is a big plus. Homes that have this access are considered far more desirable, both for owners and for potential tenants, than those that do not. Jane said that she wanted a place that was close to where Bob worked (he was an engineer in a food-processing plant), so he wouldn't have a long commute. Bob said that their house should be located somewhere between their two jobs. (Jane was a vocational nurse and worked in an assisted living facility.) Leo said that being somewhere between the two workplaces was a good idea for their first home.

"Okay," Bob said. "Let's be sure I understand what you're saying. We should look for a home with the four criteria you just described."

Criteria for a House That's Easy to Resell

1. Good neighborhood schools
2. Pride of ownership evident in the neighborhood
3. Low crime rate in the neighborhood
4. Close to shopping, and with access to transportation

"But," Bob continued, "those are things any smart person would look for when buying a home to live in. What about the special features you mentioned that are peculiar just to *investment* homes?"

Leo nodded. "Since real estate investments have to be rented out to produce income, any home that you purchase should have qualities that also make it a good rental. Remember," Leo said, "in some markets, particularly when prices are falling and there's a large inventory, you may not be able to resell quickly. Therefore, you'll want to hold the property and rent it out. Here are additional things to look for in a rental house."

"Rental House" Criteria

Minimum/Maximum House Size

"How big a house do you want?" Leo asked. Jane and Bob looked at each other. "Big enough for us to feel comfortable," Jane said. "But not too big, so that it costs a lot," Bob added.

Leo said that most people feel the same way. That preference usually translates into at least three bedrooms and two baths with a minimum of about 1,800 to 2,000 square feet. "You'll be comfortable in a house that size, and chances are that most others will be too when it comes time to resell.

"More important, you should find lots of tenants who would be willing to rent a house of that size."

"Really?" asked Bob. "I always thought a bigger house would rent better—you could get more people into it."

Leo nodded. "Generally speaking, as you say, a bigger house will rent faster and for more money because more people can live in it. You'll usually be able to rent a house with five bedrooms faster than a smaller home.

"The trouble is that the bigger the house and the greater the number of people in it, the more wear and tear there is on it. You want a house that's big enough to get a good rental rate, but isn't so big that you'll attract tenants with huge families.

"According to the Fair Housing Act, you can't refuse to rent to families with children. But children, by their nature, tend to be rougher on a home. And the house size will determine how many children will fit into it. A five-bedroom house can accommodate far more kids than a four-bedroom or three-bedroom house. But five bedrooms won't generate that much more rent, and the small amount of additional rent won't compensate for the wear and tear caused by so many people living in one house. The best rental home is generally a three-bedroom house, with a four-bedroom house following. Anything more is simply asking for rental trouble."

TIP

Usually a three- or four-bedroom house is the optimum rental size—five bedrooms is too many, and two is too few.

An Active Rental Market in the Area

Leo pointed out that some areas have a lot of well-paid workers, yet a shortage of housing. This makes for an excellent tenant pool. Other areas have lots of housing, but relatively few people who want (or can afford) to live there. That's not so good.

Thus, in addition to investigating the area in which they were considering buying a home to be sure it was a good location for resale, they should also investigate to be sure that the area has a good rental market.

Bob looked skeptical. "How could we possibly know that?" he asked. Leo smiled and said, "I, or any other active agent, can quickly tell you, since most of us handle rentals as well as sales." He pointed out that Bob and Jane could also check for themselves by looking in the local paper under "homes for rent," calling some of the landlords, chatting with them, and visiting some of the rental properties. Very quickly they'd find out how well rentals were doing and what types of properties were available. "It's simply a matter of immersing yourself in the rental market until you have a feel for it."

A Sturdy, but Not Fancy House

Leo pointed out that while it is commonly believed that any home can be rented out (as indeed it can be), some homes, because of their construction, design, and amenities, make far better rentals than others. On the other hand, some homes are badly suited to be rentals.

Leo pointed out, "You usually don't want a house with expensive fixtures or features. Tenants simply don't tend to take as good care of the property as you will. Stained-glass windows, elaborate chandeliers, white carpeting, and so on are all no-no's. You want a home that will stand up to wear and tear."

Also, he pointed out, homes with pools are a rental nightmare. "Yes, as with larger-size homes, you can rent them for more. But they have increased liability and increased insurance costs. They require that you hire a pool maintenance firm. (You can't count on tenants to take good care of a pool—they might injure themselves with caustic chemicals or not apply them properly, damaging the pool and/or its equipment.) Usually the increased rent is more than offset by the cost of maintaining and repairing the pool."

TRAP

Houses with pools do rent for more. But when you factor in the additional costs of liability insurance, pool service, chemicals, equipment repair and replacement, and so on, they usually end up costing much more.

A Newer House

Finally, Leo pointed out that they would want a rental that wouldn't need a lot of upkeep and maintenance. "The expense of fixing a roof or a water heater or an air-conditioning system in an older home can turn a profitable rental into an 'alligator.'"

Both Jane and Bob laughed. It was Leo's turn to look surprised, "You haven't heard of real estate alligators? An alligator is what you have when the expenses (mortgage payment, taxes, maintenance, and repairs) on your rental property are so high that they require you to take money out of your pocket each month just to keep the property afloat. It becomes an alligator that eats you alive."

Your goal is to at least break even. That means that the rent (plus tax advantages—see Chapter 7) pays for all (or almost all) your expenses.

TRAP

Most investors tend to downplay the costs of repair and maintenance when buying a property. Unfortunately, when these costs turn out to be unexpectedly high, they can turn a dream home into a nightmare. That's why newer homes requiring generally fewer repairs are better investments.

"But all homes require some repair and maintenance," Bob pointed out sternly.

"True," Leo said. "But the younger the home, the less likely it is that it will need work." He explained that homes less than seven years old rarely need to have water heaters or anything else replaced. Homes less than 15 years old rarely require new roofs, extensive work on heating/air-conditioning systems, and so on. He said that the ideal rental property is less than 15 years old, and preferably less than 7.

"Okay," said Jane. "To summarize, that means that we're looking for a home that also has the four additional criteria you just described."

Criteria of a House That's Easy to Rent

1. Not too big/not too small
2. An active rental market in the area

3. A house that is suitable for tenants
4. A house that is easily maintained without lots of repairs

Make It Suitable for Someone Else

Leo nodded. But Bob had a scowl on his face. "What you're really saying," he began, "is that everything we look for has to be suitable for someone else—the next buyer or a tenant. What if we find something that we like for ourselves that falls outside these criteria? Can't we please ourselves first?"

Jane looked surprised and asked what Bob meant. He replied that suppose they found a cute little home that was perfect for them. It had two or five bedrooms. It had some ornate wooden banisters. It had expensive white carpeting and fancy imported tile work in the kitchen. It was 40 years old. It wasn't in a great school district. And so on. In short, while it might make a perfect home for them, it might not be suitable for tenants or for later resale.

"What you're saying is that we need to give up some of what we want to have in order to buy a property that will be better suited to investing." Jane looked shocked. "I don't want to buy a home for someone else—I want to buy one for us!" Bob nodded.

Jane and Bob looked questioningly at Leo. Leo hunched his shoulders and said, "It's your decision. Do you want comfort and satisfaction right now? Or are you willing to wait until you have amassed a real estate fortune?

"While some compromise is possible, if you're truly an investor, then you'll first look at the investment criteria in any property you buy."

"How much compromise is possible?" Jane asked.

"Some, but not a lot," Leo said. "At some point you've got to bite the bullet and buy for investment."

The whole idea of investing in real estate is to sacrifice some of the things you want during the first few years so that after that time, you'll have enough investment profits to buy anything you want. Instead of buying the home of your dreams, you compromise and buy a home that you can stand to live in, and that later will make a good rental and sale. Remember, you're not going to stay there forever.

Jane looked crushed, but Bob said, "Actually, that makes sense."

Jane looked at him as though he were a traitor. Leo waited a moment, then said, "Instead of worrying about a potential property, let's see if we can find an actual one—then you can decide. First off, let's make sure we understand what you don't want. You don't want a condo or a co-op."

Why Not Buy a Condo or a Co-op?

Bob seemed surprised. "We have only about $10,000. I know that's not a lot when it comes to real estate, so I was thinking we'd be better off buying a condo or a co-op, because they're cheaper."

Leo nodded. "Yes, they can be cheaper in absolute price. But, since about 2001 when the condo market took off, many of them actually cost more in price per square foot than many comparable single-family homes!"

Bob was surprised. Leo explained that condos, and to some extent co-ops, had traditionally been the stepchildren of real estate. "They were frequently the last to go up in price in a hot market, and the first to go down in a cold market." That changed in the early 2000s, when the idea of a maintenance-free lifestyle began to appeal to many people, especially empty nesters (retirees whose children had grown up and moved on). Since most condos and co-ops had all exterior maintenance handled by the homeowners' association (as well as many amenities such as a spa, pool, tennis court, and so on), they became increasingly popular.

"However," Leo said, "I definitely would *not* recommend them as a rental."

Both Bob and Jane were confused. Leo saw their confusion and continued. "Condos have a homeowners' association, or HOA, with a board of directors and an architectural committee that establish rules that often act as roadblocks to landlords. For example, the HOA might prohibit individual owners from posting 'For Rent' signs in front of the building. Often there are also parking, noise, and occupancy restrictions.

"It's important to understand," Leo said, "that a condo is not simply a cheaper house. It's a different lifestyle. Occupants usually share common walls, ceilings, and floors. They share pools and other recreation areas. The landscaping in front of the units is handled by the HOA and usually cannot be altered. You usually can't even change the exterior paint. In short, in a condo, you give up some independence for the good of the community. This shared type of lifestyle usually works best with owner-occupants who agree to live by its standards. It can be a problem, however, for tenants who don't have a vested interest in the sharing, but want only habitation and to be left alone."

Leo pointed out that co-ops are even more restrictive than condos. Often the board that governs the co-op will insist on financially approving any tenants. Sometimes, although the practice is completely illegal, their interference extends to disapproving the tenants themselves on issues of race, religion, or national origin. Some co-ops simply don't want any tenants at all in the building.

"In other words," Jane said, "we could have trouble renting out a condo or co-op."

"Sometimes even just showing such a property can be a nightmare," Leo said. "All of which is why I recommend going with single-family, detached housing, which is usually most in demand by renters and most in demand when it comes time to resell. I'm not saying that you can't successfully invest in and rent out a condo or co-op. I am saying that given a choice, I would opt for a detached house."

Jane and Bob looked at each other, and then nodded. They had agreed to follow Leo's lead, and they decided not to question it further for now. Of course, if things didn't work out in the future, they could always strike out in another direction.

"Okay," Jane said. "We'll try for a house. But, as we said, we have only about $10,000."

Leo nodded. He said, "You can probably get a 90 percent or higher mortgage, depending on your credit, so that should be enough. Of course, there are closing costs, which can add to that, but I think you'll be able to manage."

TIP

Credit *reports* are simply a statement of a person's debts and history of repayment. A credit *score* evaluates the credit report (and other information) and translates it into numerical data. Fair Isaac (FICO), the most widely used credit-scoring company, uses scores from 350 to 850. The higher the score, the better the credit.

Leo explained that in the central California area where they lived, there were plenty of homes in the $200,000 to $300,000 price range, "Especially since the last real estate slowdown hit."

"In fact," Leo said, "I would encourage you to look for a foreclosure. There are many of them on the market, and some make excellent deals for first-time investors."

Bob and Jane smiled at this. A foreclosure sounded like a perfect way to get a good deal.

Looking for a Foreclosure

The first thing Leo suggested that they do was apply for mortgage "preapproval." "You can do that with lenders such as www.eloan.com, www.quicken.com, www.lendingtree.com, or any one of many other online lenders. Or you can use a physical mortgage broker—I can give you a name. But however you do it, get preapproved first, before you do anything else."

Next he suggested that they go back to their home and use their computer to check the Internet for foreclosures. "Try www.foreclosure.com, www.realtytrac.com, www.foreclosurelistings.com, or other similar sites for a list of foreclosures in your area. The sites usually have educational articles, too, so you can read up on how to buy a foreclosure. You should find lots of properties to look at."

Bob and Jane went home. They tried several sites and found not just hundreds, but thousands of foreclosures. They were in all price ranges, all sizes, and all neighborhoods.

Jane e-mailed a couple of listings and suddenly began being bombarded with e-mails from agents offering to show her properties. It seemed overwhelming.

So Bob picked one house that was in foreclosure and called the seller from the name he got on the foreclosure Web site. The man who answered was gruff, didn't want to talk to them, and hung up.

Things didn't seem to be working out well.

The next weekend they went back to see Leo.

Leo was sympathetic. He explained that people in foreclosure were often overwhelmed with calls from agents and investors and quickly got turned off. It wasn't all that unusual to get a gruff response.

He went on to elaborate that there were three stages of foreclosures.

The Three Stages of Foreclosure

1. Preforeclosure

The first stage, Leo explained, comes about when a borrower fails to make payments for a few months. The lender then sends the borrower (and records) a formal document called a "notice of default." It explains how much money the borrower is in arrears and demands that it be paid. If the money is not paid, the lender explains, it will be forced sell the property at a later date to recoup the mortgage.

"Can a lender really do that?" Jane asked.

"Yes, and unfortunately it happens far too often," Leo replied. "Prices can fall, mortgages can reset to high interest rates and payments, and people can have personal troubles and be unable to make the payments or resell. All of these things tend to result in foreclosures."

Leo went on to explain that when the borrower is sent the notice of default, he or she is actually said to be in "preforeclosure." It's before the lender sells the property. "This is the time that most investors feel you can get the best bargains," he added.

Jane and Bob nodded.

TIP

Most real estate investors prefer to deal in preforeclosures with prices lower than the median price for homes in the area. The reason is that they are easier to buy (less financing), and they usually offer a bigger tenant and resale base.

2. Auction Sale

The second stage is when the property is auctioned at a foreclosure sale. There may be a court-ordered sale, which happens in states such as Florida that have judicial foreclosure. Or a trustee can auction the property right on the courthouse steps in trust deed states, such as California. (Web sites such as www.foreclosure.com usually list what type of state you're in.) Anyone can bid, but usually the lender bids the full price of the mortgage plus accrued interest and penalties and wins the auction.

"You don't want to mess with an auction sale," Leo said, "until you become sophisticated investors. It's often difficult to inspect such properties, you may have trouble finding out how much is actually owed (the number and value of different mortgages), and the other bidders can be very clever and tricky."

3. Real Estate Owned

The final stage is after the lender gets the property at auction and now wants to resell it. These properties are called "real estate owned" or "REOs" by the lender. Typically the lender will fix up the properties (if they are in disrepair) and list them with a local agent. You can buy them through the agent just the same way you would if you were buying from an individual seller. However, because the lender usually wants market price, you can have more difficulty getting a bargain here. (Though it's not impossible—see later in this chapter.)

"So, from what you're saying, we want to work with a property in the preforeclosure stage," Jane said.

Leo nodded. "That's when you're likely to get a good deal. And Web sites usually break down the properties by preforeclosure, auction, and REOs, so it's easy to find those properties.

"But," Leo went on, "you'll be dealing with people who are scared, because they've gotten their notice of default. And who are angry because of all the calls, e-mails, and letters they've gotten from agents and other investors. (They're often also angry at themselves for having gotten into their current predicament.) That's probably why you got such a gruff response when you called. So, while this provides the best pickings for investment, it's also not easy."

"But," Bob asked, "it's where we're most likely to get bargains, right?"

Leo nodded.

"But, you'll help us, right?"

Leo hesitated. "When you buy a preforeclosure, the seller typically gets little, if anything, out of the deal. Hence, there probably won't be a commission in it for me. So, quite frankly, I won't want to do most of the grunt work.

"However, I'll give you all the advice and help that I can, on the understanding that when you close, you'll pay me $1,000 as a commission. And also on the 'gentleman's agreement' that when you resell, you'll list with me. I know you're just getting started, and I want to encourage you. Hopefully, the better you do down the road, the more commissions will be in it for me."

Bob and Jane looked at each other, then shook hands with Leo.

The Preforeclosure on Sycamore Street

Jane scoured the Internet foreclosure sites for preforeclosures. First, she limited her search to homes in neighborhoods near where she and Bob lived, feeling that she understood those areas best. Also, she looked for homes in the same school district, a good one, so that Renee, their daughter, wouldn't have to change schools.

She was also able to use Internet foreclosure sites to direct her to information that identified preforeclosures in terms of the crime potential for the neighborhood, the age of the property, the size, and so on. The final result was a home on Sycamore Street that, at least from the online stats, seemed just right.

So, she and Bob went out to see the owners. The house itself appeared run-down from the outside. Screens were missing from windows or torn; the paint was faded in places and peeling in others. The lawn had gone yellow and died, probably from lack of watering.

It seemed a wreck of a house; nevertheless, they knocked on the door and introduced themselves. Ivan, who answered, seemed flabbergasted. "You're one of those investors looking to steal my place, aren't you?" he said.

Bob was nonplussed. "We're not looking to steal anything," he replied. "We're looking for an investment property to buy. If yours fits the bill, all the better for both of us."

"No matter, no matter," Ivan said. "I've gotten hundreds of calls, e-mails, and flyers, but you're the first people who actually came by. Come on in and let's talk!"

Ivan introduced his wife, Teresa, and the couples sat down in the living room. Jane began by saying that she had heard that the property was in foreclosure.

Ivan bristled and said, "You probably saw it on one of those Web sites, didn't you?!"

Teresa put a hand on Ivan's arm, and he calmed immediately.

"Yes, we did," Bob said. "Is that a problem?"

Ivan explained that once they got the notice of default, the Web sites had picked up their property, and everyone seemed to know about it. "No matter, no matter," he said. "We have to sell anyway."

Then he went on to tell their story. Ivan said that they had listed the property for sale for three months, but had been unable to find a buyer. The trouble was that they had gotten a no-down-payment mortgage with a very low interest rate and very low payments. However, those were only for three years, and that time was up. Now the mortgage had reset to almost double the interest rate, and their payments had almost doubled. "There's no way can we make payments like that!" Ivan said. Teresa nodded and said, "We tried to sell, but we were told that the initial low interest rate was only a 'teaser.' The actual rate was much higher, and the difference was being added to our mortgage each month. Now we owe $40,000 more than we originally borrowed!"

"Yes," Ivan continued, "and with the housing slump in this area, our home's price went down, so now we owe more than the house is worth. That's why it wouldn't sell. Now we can't make the payments and can't sell, so we're going to lose the place to the finance company. The worst thing is that it will ruin our credit, so we won't be able to buy another home."

Bob and Jane commiserated with Ivan and Teresa. They explained that they were new to the business and didn't really know what they might be able to do. But they had a friend, an agent, who might be able to come up with an answer if anyone could. They went back to see Leo.

When they explained the situation, he nodded. "Their mortgage payment is higher because after three years the interest rate reset to a much higher rate. Also, they had negative amortization. In their case, the low payments meant that instead of the loan going down each month, the discounted interest they were not paying was added to the loan, so it went up.

"In trade talk," Leo said, "They are 'upside down.' They owe more than their property's worth. Their only hope, and yours, is for a 'short sale,' where the lender is willing to take less than it is owed."

"Will a lender actually do that?" Jane asked.

"Maybe," Leo said. "But before pursuing that, what do you think of the property? If you could get it, would it make a good investment?"

Jane and Bob looked at each other. "We think so," Jane said. "It fits all the criteria for both a resale and a rental that we discussed earlier—good schools, right size, good tenant market, and so on. The only problem with it is that it's run-down. It needs lots of work."

"A fixer-upper, in other words," Leo said.

They both nodded.

"Okay," Leo began. "Here's what you need to do. There are really two big steps."

Working with a Fixer-Upper

Step 1

"First, you need to find out if you can make a profit. That means you need to determine what price you should pay for the house. That has to factor in all the costs of fixing it up."

Bob said that he had gone to www.zillow.com, a Web site that gave values free for properties, and found that other *similar* homes in the area had been selling in the $240,000 price range.

"Okay," Leo said. "Your CMA (comparative market analysis—comparison with recent resales) gave you a retail price. We'll assume that's what the house will sell for when it's all fixed up and in good shape. (In a down housing market, you need to discount this amount in order to account for falling prices.) "Now, you have to calculate as accurately as possible how much it will cost to fix it up. Then you subtract the cost of fixing it up from the retail price. You should also subtract the cost of paying a $1,000 short commission to me. That will give you your *wholesale* price, or what you should pay for the property."

Step 2

"Next, you should contact the lender and find out if it will accept that low price. If it will, then you have the makings of a good deal."

Bob and Jane left feeling uplifted. They felt they were on the way. They went back to Ivan and Teresa and explained that they needed to determine how much their fix-up costs would be, and then they needed to go see the lender to work out a deal.

Ivan and Teresa were hopeful. This was the first positive thing that had happened to them in months. Ivan explained that they were now over 130 days delinquent on their payments. "When we couldn't make the whole payment, we just stopped making any," he said

Teresa looked embarrassed about the condition of the property and said, "It hardly seemed worthwhile taking care of the place when we figured we would lose it."

At that point, Bob interjected, "You said you were 130 days delinquent. How much time do you actually have left?"

"The foreclosure auction's in two weeks," Ivan replied.

Bob looked at Jane, and she said, "We'd better get going then."

Bob and Jane made notes about everything they figured needed to be done to fix up the place. Some of the work, such as painting and landscaping, they could do themselves. They'd hire out fixing broken things like screens, windows, doors, holes in the walls, and so on. Fortunately, all of the systems (heating, air conditioning, plumbing, electrical, and so on) worked, as far as they could tell.

"We should get a professional inspection," Jane said. Bob nodded, but said, "I don't think there's enough time."

It was Friday before they had all the information. They had called contractors and checked with building supply outlets to get prices. They called Leo and factored in a commission. He told them to add an additional 2 or 3 percent for closing costs. The final number was $54,000 in costs. They subtracted that from an estimated market price of $240,000 and came up with a purchase price of $186,000.

"How much do they owe?" Bob asked. Jane replied, "I forgot to ask." So she called Ivan, who said that their loan balance, including interest and fees, was $251,000. He also said that he had called the lender, as they had instructed, and a meeting was set for the following Monday at 9 a.m.

When she hung up and told Bob how much they owed, he whistled in surprise. "We would be offering to buy the place for $65,000 less than the loan balance! The lender will never agree to that." So they called Leo.

Why the Lender Might Do It

Leo listened to all their figures and then said, "The lender will do only what's to the lender's advantage. If there's a good reason for the lender to take so much less, it very well may. (Some lenders simply won't listen to reason, but others will.)

"What you have to do is provide the reasons for the lender to make the deal. I can help you there with some information."

They went down to Leo's office, and he explained.

"Lenders are in the business of making loans. When they have a performing mortgage, it's an asset. However, when the borrower doesn't make payments, as is the case with Teresa and Ivan, the loan becomes a 'nonperforming' mortgage. And when the lender forecloses, the property becomes an REO. A nonperforming loan and an REO are considered liabilities.

"Furthermore, the government insists that many lenders set aside capital reserves for nonperforming loans and REOs in case the property is eventually disposed of for less than the loan amount. Sometimes these reserves for REOs can be as high as 50 percent of the loan amount. That's the case when there is a down market and little is selling.

"Therefore, the lender naturally doesn't want a nonperforming mortgage and really doesn't want an REO.

"Of course, lenders always anticipate some foreclosures and set up reserves to handle them. However, we're in a down market now, and there are thousands of foreclosures on the market. Those reserves are probably pushed to the limit and may even be long gone. Let's see how many foreclosures the lender currently has on the books. What is the lender's name?"

Bob said it was the Bank of John Smith—a small, local bank.

Leo nodded. "Their REOs are all handled by ZYX Realty. I'm friendly with them. Let me make a call."

Leo was on the phone for a few minutes. When he got off, he said, "The bank has over 270 foreclosures for sale right now in this market. It told the agent that it is desperate for sales because the bank regulators are hot on its heels with concerns about solvency. (Too many foreclosures, too many capital reserve requirements, and the bank could go under.)

"I think you might be able to make a deal. Here's what you do.

1. "Tell the bank that the sellers haven't been able to move the preforeclosure, even though they have had it listed for three months.

2. "Point out that they currently owe far more than the preforeclosure is worth.

3. "Show the lender your estimated costs, including fix-up costs, commission to resell, and so forth, and explain how you came up with your price.

4. "Tell the bank that you'll take the property off its hands immediately, for your price."

"But," Bob asked, "how do we come up with the $186,000 purchase price if the bank agrees?"

Leo smiled. "Remember that I asked you to get *preapproved*. Did you do it?"

Jane nodded. "Then call your preapproval lender and explain the situation. Say that you need 100 percent financing and explain the exact situation. See what the lender says. Then go see the bank on Monday."

Negotiating a "Short Sale"

On Monday, Ivan called to say that he wouldn't meet them at the bank as previously agreed. He said he was so angry with the lender that he might say something that would ruin any possible deal. But he wished them luck. So Bob and Jane went alone.

They were escorted into an office that had the title "Vice President" on the door and were introduced to Juan. "He's a VP," Bob said. Jane saw that Bob was intimidated and said, "Almost every officer in a bank is a vice president—don't let it throw you." Bob nodded.

Juan had them sit in front of his desk and then said, "Okay, what have you got for me?"

Bob explained they wanted to buy the property on Sycamore Street. He explained that that Ivan and Teresa hadn't been able to sell it because they were upside down. He also explained about the poor condition of the property, and he said that they had done a workup of the costs of fixing up the home.

Juan nodded and asked to see their work sheet. As Bob passed it over, Jane glanced at it. She was shocked to see that Bob had increased the fix-up costs by $10,000 to $64,000 and reduced the amount they were offering to pay to $176,000. She looked questioningly at Bob.

He had a crooked smile on his face and whispered to her, "We forgot to add our profit in. I just did that."

When Juan got to the bottom figure, the offering price, he chuckled. "No way," he said. "No way. You're trying to steal this property."

Bob shook his head. "Nope. It's just business. You're into a home for far more than its value. The reason is mainly the interest rate reset and the negative amortization on your loan.

"Now you have a choice. You can take our offer and immediately be done with the property. Or you can go through the further expense of a foreclosure sale, fix it up yourself, and pay an agent to sell it as an REO. But if you do, you'll be out the additional interest on the mortgage during the time all that takes. Not to mention the headache and capital reserves it will tie up. Also note that many of our costs involve us doing the work. You'll have to pay someone for the labor we'll supply. As a result, your costs will almost certainly be higher."

Juan looked directly at Bob. He didn't say anything for a few moments, then asked, "How soon can you close?"

Jane chimed in, "We're preapproved and our lender is ready to fund as soon as we get an appraisal."

Juan nodded. "I'll have to take this before the committee. I'll get back to you." He stood to leave.

"When?" Bob asked.

Juan looked down at Bob. "It could take a few weeks."

TRAP

Recently with so many properties offered for sale, lenders have been swamped and have taken weeks, sometimes months, to render a decision. A savvy investor will pressure the lender not only on price, but on time.

Bob said, "We don't have that much time—and neither does the bank. We have other properties we're working on. And the foreclosure auction is scheduled for next week."

Juan sat back down. "How much time do I have?" he asked.

"One day," said Bob. Jane sucked in her breath, but said nothing.

"You're really squeezing me," said Juan.

Bob smiled. "It's just business."

"I'll get back to you by the end of today," Juan said and got up and left. Bob and Jane walked out, too. On the way out of the bank, Jane said, "How did you know to give him only one day?"

Bob replied, "If we gave him more time, he'd just hold out hoping that some other, better offer would come in, which it might. Better we demand that he make an immediate decision." Jane nodded in admiration.

Financing the Property

Juan called them back at quarter to five and said that they had a deal, provided they could close within one week. He was having the sales agreement drawn up, and they could sign it the next morning. Bob agreed.

Jane immediately called the lender and asked for an appraisal. The lender said that could take two weeks. She said she had only two days. The lender hemmed and hawed and finally agreed, but said they might have to pay an extra amount for the quick appraisal. (They didn't—appraisers were in plentiful supply now that the market had turned down.)

They got their loan. [It was a special program by the Federal National Mortgage Association (Fannie Mae) for fixer-uppers that lenders sometimes offered.] The appraiser came up with a value *after the house was fixed up* of $240,000.

From that was subtracted a 20 percent down payment, or $48,000, leaving a balance of $192,000. Of that amount, they would receive $176,000 immediately—enough for the short payoff. Then, after the fix-up work was done, they would get another $16,000.

Financing the House on Sycamore Street

After fix-up value	$240,000
Immediate funding	176,000 (purchase price)
Balance paid after fix-up work done	16,000
Mortgage	$192,000

TIP

Fannie Mae is a secondary lender that buys mortgages from primary lenders, such as banks. It has a wide variety of programs, including low-down-payment, nothing-down, sweat-equity, and fix-up loans. A good mortgage broker can introduce you to all its programs. The Federal Home Loan Mortgage Association (Freddie Mac) is a similar organization with its own set of programs.

Before signing the contract, Bob took it back to Leo, who suggested a few changes. Then Bob took it to Ivan and Teresa. After all, they were the sellers of the home.

Negotiating with the Sellers

Ivan read it over and then snorted, "I told you that you were stealing the property. There's nothing here for us!"

"Not really," Bob shrugged. "By the time we get everything fixed, we'll make only $10,000. That's reasonable for our efforts."

Ivan nodded, then demanded, "But what about me? What do I get out of it?"

Bob waited a moment and then asked, "What did you put in? You bought the property for nothing down. And you've lived here now for nearly six months without making a payment—essentially rent free.

"More important, this is a legitimate sale. It will help save your credit. You won't have a foreclosure against you. That means you'll probably be able to go out and buy another house."

Teresa nodded. But Ivan looked slyly at Bob. "I had to pay closing costs when I bought," he said. "What about those?"

"I'll have to pay closing costs, too." Bob said.

Ivan looked deflated. Bob offered, "I know it's hard losing your house. But it's a good deal. And I'll throw in $500 cash to help with your move."

"Make it a thousand," Ivan said. Bob nodded, and the deal was done.

Many states have special laws that apply when someone buys a home from a seller who's in preforeclosure. They usually provide an "equity of redemption." That means that the seller can come back for a period of time, often as long as a year or more, and reclaim the home by paying off all the costs of the buyer/investor. Furthermore, the buyer/investor may be precluded from reselling or renting the property during that time period. Check with a good attorney for the rules in your state.

Fixing Up the Sycamore Street Preforeclosure

Buying the house cost Jane and Bob $3,500 in closing costs. In addition, they paid $1,000 to Leo and another $1,000 to Ivan and Teresa. A regular escrow was run, and they obtained title insurance.

When they moved in, they had a home that was a wreck and a little less than $5,000 in cash to work with. So the first thing they did was apply for a home equity loan. Home equity loans are limited to a maximum of 80 percent of the property's value. But because their mortgage was so low, they were able to secure a $10,000 loan. Using that money and their savings, they began fixing up the property.

They did the heavy work first, then moved in. They then continued to fix up the property while they were living in it. That proved inconvenient, but it saved them paying both rent on an apartment and mortgage payments.

Three months later, they were finished. At that time, they applied for the $16,000 balance on their first mortgage (available when the work was done) and used that money to pay off their home equity loan and also allow them to put $6,000 in the bank.

They now had a fixed-up property that was worth $240,000 with a loan balance of $196,000. In other words, they had generated nearly $45,000 in equity.

Moving on to an REO—the House on Lexington Drive

Bob and Jane lived in the house on Sycamore Street for more than a year before they went back to see Leo. They said they were ready to rent out that house, and they wanted him to find them a new home.

This time things moved faster.

Leo said that he would find them a place, although the market had changed over the course of the year. Now, most of the pre-foreclosures had worked their way through the system and had become REOs. The lenders were absolutely desperate to get rid of them. "I think you'll be able to get a good deal on an REO," he suggested. They agreed to see.

Leo called them a few days later and said he'd come by. He took them to see a property on Lexington Drive, not far from where they lived.

TIP

When you're buying a rental (in this case, they would rent out the Sycamore Street property), always buy close to home. Try never to buy more than a half an hour away. That makes it easy for you to handle rent-up, repair, maintenance, and tenant problems personally. This actually becomes the ninth parameter.

The property was about the same size as their current home, and like theirs had been when they bought theirs, it was in terrible shape. The big difference was that it was empty and they could tour it.

Leo pointed out that the Lexington Drive home needed paint. One of the bathrooms had broken fixtures, which would need to be replaced. The electricity, gas, and water were all turned on, and it quickly became clear that the natural gas heater/air conditioner did not operate. And one of the two toilets did not flush properly.

They made a list of all of the problems with the home. Then Leo said, "You should check it out for the criteria we discussed when you bought your first home—both as a rental and for resale. But you must do it quickly.

"The lender just got this at auction. Because it has a backlog of foreclosures, the lender hasn't yet started to fix and clean. But it will within a couple of weeks. However, if you can make an 'as is' offer, you might be able to get a bargain."

Jane asked, "Does an 'as is' offer mean we take it in its present condition?"

"Yes," said Leo. "However, I would suggest that you also demand that you be given a fix-up/cleanup allowance from the lender. (It'll pay you for the work as it gets done.) If the amount you ask for is less than it will cost the lender to do it, the lender might agree to go along.

"Also, I would suggest that you ask the lender to finance your purchase. Ask for a market-interest-rate mortgage for the full amount of the purchase price, but insist that the lender pay all closing costs and that there be no 'points' to you."

Bob raised his eyebrows, and Leo explained, "You probably forgot the point you paid on your last mortgage. Points are an extra charge that lenders make to increase their yield on mortgages. A point is equal to 1 percent of the loan. For example, 5 points means 5 percent of the mortgage. Most mortgages carry a few points, but that can be expensive to the buyer/borrower.

"And, because I happen to know that this lender is really desperate, I would also include a one-time assumption clause."

Both Bob and Jane looked at each other and then back at Leo. "It means," he said, "that when you resell the property, the next buyer can assume the mortgage, provided, of course, that he or she can provide a good credit report and credit score. In normal circumstances, lenders today prefer not to agree to this. They want to have the mortgage paid off and to get the fees and, if possible, a higher interest rate from a new mortgage. However, if you can get the bank to agree to an assumption clause, you will have a far easier time when it comes to reselling."

"Do you really think the lender will go along with that?" Bob questioned.

"We can only ask," Leo said. "First, however, make sure that the property is suitable both for resale and as a rental. Do your homework."

Bob and Jane did so and called Leo back two days later. "It'll work," Jane said.

"Good," Leo replied. "I thought it would. I'll come by, and we can draw up an offer."

Leo explained that REOs were typically handled through a local real estate agent, and this property was no exception. The lender was set up to pay a commission on the sale. Hence, Leo could handle the transaction for them as the buyer's agent and be paid by the lender as a cobroker. He came by, and they worked out an offer.

A CMA revealed that if the property was in good shape, it would probably be worth around $260,000 after being discounted in the current market.

Bob indicated that their best estimate was that it would cost them around $25,000 to put into shape. That meant that "as is," it was probably worth $235,000.

"But," Leo pointed out, "that's what it might be worth by the time a sale comes around. However, in today's market, we have an inventory of 10 months. That means that the typical house is on the market for 10 months before it sells. The lender will have capital reserves tied up for that period of time—not to mention the lack of interest coming in on a nonperforming mortgage. And there's also the taxes and the insurance that the lender will need to pay. Add to that the utilities required (gas, electric, and water) to keep the house cool in warm weather and warm in colder weather so that it's suitable for showing. All of that will undoubtedly cost the lender another $20,000. You'll save the lender that much money by buying it immediately 'as is.'

"And, of course, you'll be removing a headache."

"So, you're saying that we should cut the price another $20,000?"

"I'd make it $15,000," said Leo. "You should leave the lender something so that it'll want to deal with you."

"That's makes for an offer of about $220,000," Jane said. "Let's do it!"

Leo drew up the offer. "Normally," he said, "the offer would contain an inspection contingency. That would give you a couple of weeks to have a professional inspector check out the property. However, because you're buying 'as is' and because you want to entice the lender to sell to you, I suggest we leave it out. It's a definite risk, especially since there may be something seriously wrong that we didn't notice."

Bob said, "We'll take the chance." Jane offered, "We're investors now, and we have to cut some corners to get a good deal." They signed, and Leo departed.

TRAP

Buying without an inspection is definitely risky. If nothing is wrong with the house, it could help you get a bargain. But, if there's a serious hidden defect you don't consider, it could cost you big bucks, too.

He called back the next day around noon. "The lender didn't like your offer on the Lexington Drive property."

Bob and Jane were crushed. "Why?" asked Jane.

Leo explained that the lender didn't object to the cleanup allowance or paying for closing costs and points. It even went along with the reduced price. But it balked at the assumption clause, and it really didn't like carrying back the mortgage, although it agreed to do so. The officer he had talked with had said that the bank wanted to be done with the property. It didn't like the idea of someone carrying back a mortgage and then having the buyers (Bob and Jane) not be able to make the payments and have the property fall back into foreclosure. The last thing it wants is to take that property back.

"Let's leave the assumption clause out," Bob said. "When it's time to sell it, I'm sure we can find someone who can qualify for a new mortgage. If not, we can always rent it out."

Leo said that probably would work, but he had another idea. Since the lender was insistent on not having to worry about getting the property back, what if Bob and Jane went out and got their own financing? Everything else would be the same, except that the lender would be free and clear of the property as soon as the sale was concluded.

Jane, who was listening in on the extension, said, "I'm sure we can do that. Before we came to see you, we called the same online mortgage broker we used before and got preapproved again. Only this time our credit score is much higher. I guess owning a home helped."

Bob then added, "Shouldn't getting outside financing be worth something to the lender, since we're already removing the assumption clause?"

Leo agreed, then asked, "How much do you think it's worth?"

"Say a further $10,000 price reduction?" Bob replied.

Leo chuckled over the phone and said, "I'll draw up a new purchase agreement, and we'll see."

Leo came by with the new offer. It specified that they would get outside financing and also contained a contingency clause that said that if they couldn't get the financing, they wouldn't be required to go through with the deal.

They signed. Leo picked up a copy of their preapproval letter, and then he went back to see the lender.

He called two hours later. "You've got yourself a deal!"

Moving In

Jane and Bob moved into the Lexington Drive property and fixed it up while they were living there. At the same time, they rented out their old home on Sycamore Street. That way they didn't have to worry about making two mortgage payments.

They used their old revolving home equity loan on the Sycamore Street property, which was still in place, to borrow the money they needed to fix up their new home on Lexington Drive. It took them six months to do the work a little bit at a time, then they refinanced with a new first mortgage that paid off both their existing first loan and their home equity loan. The new single mortgage had far lower payments than the two old loans.

They spent another six months personalizing the property, making it just the way they liked it. In fact, they ended up with a home they liked so much that they decided not to move again. Their daughter, Renee, liked the school, they liked the neighbors, and the shopping and recreation in the area suited their needs perfectly. So when they went back to see Leo a little over a year after buying the home on Lexington Drive, they told him that they wanted to do things differently.

Trading Up

"This time," Jane said, "We want to keep the house we're living in. We want to stay there. Is there any way we can do that and still go out and buy another property?"

Leo smiled. "Where there's a will, there's always a way," he replied. "Remember, you now own two properties, one of them a rental. What you can do now is trade up the rental on Sycamore Street. It's been two years since you bought it, and you should have a sizable equity."

"So what you're saying," Bob reiterated, "is that we should sell the first home on Sycamore Street and then use the funds to buy a new home, right?"

CAUTION

The following discussion is designed to provide a basic overview of real estate taxation and especially Section 1031 exchanges. It is limited in detail, and you should not rely on it. For more information on tax-free exchanges, see Chapter 4. For tax advice, consult with a professional.

Leo shook his head. "Not exactly. What I'm suggesting is a tax-deferred exchange. You've been renting the property on Sycamore Street for at least a year, so it's no longer considered your personal residence by the IRS. Now it's an investment property. As such, it qualified for special treatment by the IRS—a 1031 exchange."

TRAP

After converting a personal residence to an investment property, you must normally rent that property out for at least a year and a day before it qualifies for a 1031 exchange—check with your tax professional.

"What's the advantage of trading?" Jane asked.

"Tax deferral," Leo replied. "In real estate, there's always tax to pay on your profit. For example, let's say that you would have a capital gain of $100,000 if you sold your Sycamore Street rental outright. There would be both federal and state capital gains taxes to pay on that amount. That would be a maximum of 15 percent for the feds *plus* whatever your state charged you.

TIP Some Web sites offer a comparison of the tax savings from doing a tax-deferred exchange rather than simply selling and rebuying. My favorite is www.1031vest.com.

"So what you're saying," Jane said, thinking aloud, "is that if we simply sell and then reinvest, we'll lose a lot of our capital to taxes. On the other hand, if we do an exchange, we can use all that money that we would otherwise have paid in taxes to reinvest in our new property."

"Exactly," said Leo. "You'll end up with more equity as well as a bigger new property. The tax-deferred exchange is one of the great advantages offered by real estate."

"Hold on a second," said Bob. "I thought it was called a 'tax-free' exchange. You're calling it 'tax-deferred.' That doesn't sound like the same thing."

Leo smiled. "Laymen often refer to it as 'tax-free,' by which they mean that there's no tax due at the time of the sale. However, technically the tax isn't forgiven, it's simply deferred into the future. I always like to refer to it by the proper terminology, tax-deferred. That describes the situation more clearly. Remember, your tax basis in your old property is transferred to your new property. Thus, were you to eventually resell your new property outright for a profit, you'd still owe the old capital gains."

"So, we're not really saving any tax money, then. We're just pushing it into the future," said Jane.

"Think of it this way," Leo said. "The power of a traditional IRA (individual retirement account) is that *all* of the money you put in is continually reinvested—it's not taxed until you take it out. Thus you get the power of investing *all* of your capital.

"The situation here is similar. All of your capital is reinvested in real estate, and you can continue to do tax-deferred exchanges time after time into the future. There's no tax to pay unless and until you eventually decide to sell outright. Some people never sell outright, instead exchanging over and over again and building more and more wealth in real estate."

"So, we can never get our money out—is that what you're saying?" demanded Jane.

"Not at all," Leo replied. "After you've completed the tax-deferred exchange, you can refinance the new property to get your money out up to a lender's normal limits. Refinancing normally has no effect on the tax situation of the property."

Bob and Jane nodded. They were beginning to understand the advantages of trading up.

"Let's do it," Bob said. "All we have to do now is find someone who wants to trade their property for our old home on Sycamore Street, right?"

Leo smiled again. "Nope. All you have to do is to find a buyer, any buyer, for the Sycamore Street property. Then you have to declare that you're doing a Section 1031 tax-free exchange. You will have 45 days after concluding your sale in which to identify a property that you wish to buy as part of the exchange, and 180 days in which to close the deal."

TRAP

The timelines for an exchange run concurrently. They cannot be extended.

Delayed Exchange

"Hold on," Bob said. "How can it be an exchange if we don't take title to the property that our buyer is selling? It's not an exchange at all. It's a separate sale and purchase, which you said was taxable."

"It's technically called a 'delayed' exchange," Leo explained. "The rules were hammered out decades ago in a series of court challenges. Today, it's quite common. Yes, it is in effect a separate sale and purchase. However, if you declare that it's an exchange and follow the rules exactly, you get to defer the taxes that you would otherwise have paid in the year of sale."

"So," said Jane, "we can sell our home and then go out and buy any other home?"

"It's even better than that," said Leo. "You can go out and buy any other property of 'like kind.'"

Like-Kind Property

"I get it," said Bob. "'Like kind' means it's the same kind of property. We could exchange for an apartment building because it's still residential. We aren't limited to a house."

Leo smiled kindly. "You're close," he said. "'Like kind' means any other property held for investment or business purposes. Yes, it could be an apartment building. Or it could be a commercial development, or an industrial building, or an office building, or a motel, or even bare land. Anything will do, as long the property qualifies as being held for investment or business purposes."

TRAP

It's important to understand what types of properties are *not* considered "like kind" when exchanging investment real estate. These include:

- Any property that you acquire with the purpose of immediate resale
- Your personal residence
- Partnerships
- Bonds, stocks, and other securities
- Other kinds of property, such as inventories

"Wow!" Bob whistled. "That opens up a whole new world of investing." Leo nodded.

Bob and Jane signed a listing with Leo to sell their home on Sycamore Street. What with their low purchase price, sweat equity, and appreciation over two years, they figured to net out close to $115,000.

Leo also said that he would look for a new property for them as part of the exchange. They said they were ready to move up to something different, so he would look at commercial as well as residential units.

Trading Properties

Things happened fast after that. Leo put a sign on their Sycamore Street property, listed it on the MLS® (Multiple Listing Service®), and made sure it appeared on www.realtors.com. It was also picked up on other Web sites such as www.aol.com and www.yahoo.com. In addition, he saw that it was advertised in the newspaper and appeared on his own company's Web site.

TIP

When properties are listed on the MLS, they normally also appear on www.realtors.com, probably the most widely read real estate listing Web site. Many of those properties are also picked up by other Web sites, such as those of AOL and Yahoo. This is the way to get maximum exposure, particularly since over 75 percent of home buyers check the Internet first.

It took six and a half weeks before they got a buyer. Leo presented Bob and Jane with the offer from the buyer's broker, and after some negotiating, they accepted. After commission and closing costs, they ended up with a net of close to $115,000. Bob and Jane used an intermediary (an independent third party who holds title and funds; see Chapter 4) to facilitate the 1031 tax-deferred exchange.

As far as the buyers of Bob and Jane's house were concerned, the 1031 exchange was invisible to them. They planned to move into the house on Sycamore Street and went ahead with their purchase in the normal fashion.

TRAP

The exchange must be a whole. You can't do the exchange after you've transferred title to your old property to your buyer. Taking funds from that sale yourself and trying to use them to buy a new property as part of an exchange would nullify the deal's tax-deferred status.

As soon as their home was sold, Bob and Jane began looking for a new property. (They had 45 days to identify the exchange property.) Leo showed them a small strip mall, an industrial building, and a board-and-care assisted-living home. (This was a house that had been converted so that six elderly residents could live there.) None of these appealed to them.

Then Leo showed them a small office building. It had only nine offices, and all but three of them were currently rented. Leo explained, "In most areas, the market for office space tends to be cyclical. For a while there's lot of space available as builders put up new offices. Soon there's a surplus, and prices freeze or even decline. Builders shift to other projects, and few new office projects are started.

"Eventually the demand catches up with the supply. The surplus turns into a shortage, and prices shoot up. Soon, builders, seeing the higher prices, begin building new office space, and the cycle starts over.

"The idea is to catch the bottom of the cycle, when there's a surplus of office space and prices are low, then ride it up until there's a shortage and sell for a profit."

"Doesn't the overall economy enter into it?" asked Jane.

"Certainly," said Leo. "You're unlikely to see an office space boom during an economic bust. What often happens is that the office space cycle tends to follow the general economic cycle. Right now we're near the bottom of office space prices; that's why I think it's a good time to buy, if you can afford to hold on until times change."

Bob and Jane nodded. It seemed to make sense.

The 12th Street Office Building

The office building was 14 years old, and it was on a side street off a main business thoroughfare. There were a variety of small businesses leasing office space, including a psychiatrist and a computer software consultant. What Jane liked most about the building was that it had a cute entryway with flowers and shrubs. It looked more like the entrance of a luxury apartment complex than of an office building. It had none of the stark simplicity of many of today's commercial buildings.

"Appearance counts," Leo said. "Often how well office space does is determined not only by its location, and this is a fine location, but also by its appearance."

"But if that's so," Bob noted, "how come there are three vacancies? A third of the building is vacant."

Leo explained, "Good management is key to operating a successful commercial property. The owner is retired and simply doesn't have the time to do a good job of management. He's seldom here; he just posts a sign out in back, and if someone wants to rent, they have to call him. Lately, with the surplus office space available around town, there haven't been many calls. Hence the vacancies.

"On the other hand, if you were more aggressive about renting—took out ads, came around more often, and posted a good-looking sign out front—I'd wager you could fill it up."

"How much does he want for the place?" Jane asked.

"Over a million dollars," said Leo. "However, he'll have to sell for the appraisal, and that will depend on the cap rate."

Bob and Jane looked at each other. "Cap rate?"

Leo explained. "Most commercial property is evaluated in terms of its cash flow," he said. "Once you determine the cash flow, you can determine the rate of return on the investment. It's the same sort of thing you would do if you were buying any other investment, from bonds to stocks. The rate of return is expressed as the 'cap,' or capitalization rate. (This is called the income approach to evaluation.) It's relatively easy to calculate, *provided the cash flow is verifiable*. (See also Chapter 6 for a more detailed explanation.)

"To find the cap rate, you take the gross income (before debt expense), subtract all operating and vacancy expenses, and divide by the price of the property.

"For example, this property, in its current shape with three vacancies, has a net operating income of $72,000 annually. Cap rates in the range of 8 to 9 percent are what most investors in this area are looking for today. (The cap rate that investors find acceptable is one that competes favorably with other types of investments, such as CDs, stocks, bonds, and so forth.) When we divide $72,000 by 8 percent, we come up with a price of $900,000.

"Of course," Leo noted, "the seller wants more. He's projecting what the building would be worth if it were 100 percent occupied and brought in $108,000 annually. At an 8 percent cap rate, that would make the building worth $1,350,000. But he's not likely to get that."

Bob took the bait and asked, "Why not?"

"Because," Leo continued, "commercial real estate is all about the financing. Remember that I earlier said *verifiable* cash flow?" They nodded.

"That's what lenders look at—and this building has had three vacancies for over a year. As far as any lender is concerned, the verifiable cash flow is $72,000, not $108,000. And that translates into about a $900,000 price."

"So what you're saying," Bob went on, "is that the seller can't get a higher price because financing for it isn't available."

Leo nodded. "Maybe it would be if office space in the market were in short supply. But right now, it's in surplus. So if he wants to sell, he has to cut his price. And for you, that means a good deal."

Jane and Bob looked at each other and nodded. They told Leo to proceed with making an offer.

The Devil Is in the Details

Leo said that first they had to check out at least three other areas:

1. How suitable was the property for the 1031 exchange?
2. What were the leases like?
3. How strong were the tenants?

Additional Exchange Conditions

"There are several methods of identifying properties that you may want to exchange for. Most investors identify up to three (the maximum using this method) and then try to close on one. The problem, of course, is tying up three properties. We'll look at other properties, but if you like this one, I suggest that we focus on it while you continue to look. The only problem would be if you couldn't close on it in time. Remember, you have 180 days to close, but only 45 days to identify your properties."

(There are other methods of identifying properties. See Chapter 4.)

"Also, to avoid any capital gains when exchanging, you must buy a property that's of equal or greater value with one or more mortgages of equal or greater value. That certainly won't be a problem here.

"Also, to avoid paying any taxes, you can't take any cash, called *boot*, out of the deal. All the equity must flow from the old property to the new. Again, I don't see any problem here."

Evaluating the Leases

Leo went on to explain that the next thing they needed to do was to look at the leases. "Office space is leased at so much a square foot. The leases can be anything from a gross lease, where the tenant pays only the rent, to a 'triple net lease,' where the tenant not only pays rent, but is also responsible for utilities, maintenance, and taxes. For the owner, the triple net lease is often best, because it means that the other building expenses are handled by the tenant. However, in the real world, small tenants will often agree to rent only with gross rents, or perhaps with a single net lease where they are responsible for their own utilities, and sometimes maintenance. In this building, all the leases are net, with the tenants paying their own utilities and maintenance. You're responsible for taxes.

"Another area to evaluate is the length of the leases—how long are the tenants going to be committed to renting in the building? Generally speaking, if you're allowed to raise rents during the course of the lease (say at the end of each year), a long lease is better because you've locked in your tenants. On the other hand, if the rental rates are frozen (for the term of the lease), then a shorter term is usually better for you. (When their lease expires, you can demand that the tenants sign for a new, higher rate, or move them out and bring new tenants in.)"

Good Tenants—or Bad?

"Finally," Leo concluded, "you have to ask yourself how strong the tenants are. For bigger tenants that are incorporated, you can usually get a D&B (Dun & Bradstreet report) that will tell you a lot about their financial condition. For one-person 'mom and pop' operations like you have here, a personal credit report and credit score will be helpful.

"You'll also want to gauge how long the tenants have successfully been in their current business. And you'll want to see what their gross income from the business is (to help you determine if they have enough cash flow to pay their rent)."

"That's a lot," Bob said.

Jane replied, "Yes, but it all sounds like solid advice on what to check out."

Financing the Office Building

Bob and Jane did their due diligence on the property and found out that the leases were all for two or three years, with renewal options running for an additional two years. That meant that the tenants could move at the end of the year. It also meant that the owner could raise the rents at that time, if the market warranted it.

They also checked the credit reports that the seller had obtained on the tenants when they moved in. Fortunately, most of the tenants looked very solid, although two seemed a bit rocky. Those two were also the ones that had been in business for themselves the shortest amount of time.

Bob and Jane talked it over and decided that if they were to get the less desirable tenants out and then rerent the vacant offices (now five of them) to solid tenants, they could increase their cash flow and ultimately their equity in less than a year. They decided to go for it and called Leo.

When he came by, he said, "First, we have to figure out the financing."

"Simple," Bob said. "We'll get a nothing-down mortgage."

Leo smiled. "Financing for commercial real estate differs greatly from that for owner-occupied residential real estate. There you can indeed get something with nothing down. Here you'll get a maximum loan of only 80 percent, sometimes only 70 percent."

"But our credit score now is in the 800s," said Jane. "We've got great credit."

Leo nodded. "Most commercial investors do have great credit scores. However, the credit score is only the beginning. After that there's the 'skin,' or the amount of equity you can put into the property."

"So you're saying we have to come up with 20 percent down?" said Bob. "That's $180,000 on a $900,000 building. We've got only $115,000 in equity from the sale of our Sycamore Street house."

Leo nodded, then said, "Commercial lenders are typically banks, mortgage bankers, and sometimes private individuals. Some lenders will accept secondary financing, providing it all pencils out. What I suggest is that you try for an 80 percent first mortgage from a bank, and then a 10 percent second mortgage to be carried back by the seller. That way you need to put only 10 percent down."

Jane and Bob nodded. "That'll work," said Jane. "Our down payment will be only $90,000. And we'll have some money left for closing."

"To make the deal," Leo said, "I think the seller may pay any remainder of your closing costs."

"But do we have enough income from the building to make the payments?" Bob asked.

Leo explained that most lenders use a formula called the DSCR (debt service coverage ratio). "They want your DSCR to be at least 1.15 to 1.25."

Bob and Jane looked at each other and shook their heads.

Leo continued. "Basically, this means that you need to have $1.15 to $1.25 of net income for each dollar of debt repayment. On your $72,000 of net income, you can use only about $63,000 annually for debt repayment."

"Will that be enough?" asked Jane.

Leo did some quick calculations. "Assuming that we can get an 8 percent loan, your annual interest-only payment will be $57,600. Plus, of course, your payment on the second mortgage to the seller, which we can negotiate. It should work."

For more information on financing commercial properties, check into Chapter 6.

Leo contacted a lender, and they filled out an application. The lender was particularly concerned about their management abilities. When they explained that they owned rental property and were willing to spend the time to do things right on the office building, the air seemed to clear, and the lender eventually okayed the financing.

Management is a big concern of lenders. Most office buildings require full-time management because there are always issues of renting up, maintenance, repair, customization for new tenants, and so on. The lenders want to be sure that the owner/borrower will have someone on hand to do the management work as needed. For small buildings, that means a virtually full-time commitment from the owner.

Making the Deal

Leo wrote up the offer.

Bob and Jane waited anxiously for Leo's call. It came a few hours later. Leo said, "The seller won't take the offer. He still wants a million dollars, minimum."

Bob and Jane were both discouraged. They told Leo that it was the best offer they could make.

"It's not over yet," Leo said. "I left the offer sitting there on his kitchen counter and told him that, with your permission, we'd extend it for three more days. His agent said that he hadn't had an offer in five months. He may be tempted."

Bob and Jane said that it was okay to extend the offer, and Leo came over and got them to sign an extension. Then they waited.

At 11 o'clock at night on the third day, Leo called to say that the seller had accepted. It was celebration time.

When the deal closed, Bob and Jane's basis in the Sycamore Street property was transferred to the new property, giving them an equity of around $115,000, after financing. They had no taxes to pay immediately on the Section 1031 tax-deferred exchange.

Boosting the Value

After the deal closed, Bob and Jane immediately set out to rent up the vacant office space. Since the market was soft, it took them the better part of six months, but by advertising, using the services of agents, and paying special attention to management, they did get the property all rented out. But just about then, the two weak tenants bailed. They simply stopped paying rent and moved out, leaving no forwarding address. It took the remainder of the year to completely rent up the building.

However, when they had done so, the building was bringing in $108,000. Bob and Jane were pocketing over $30,000 a year, and their equity in the building was now close to half a million dollars.

By the end of the second year, the office space cycle had turned. Space was in short supply, and prices were rising. By the end of the third year, they were able to increase their rents by a third. The building began producing $144,000 in income, of which they were able to pocket over $70,000 annually.

Best of all, however, their equity based on the cap rate was now a million dollars. They refinanced, pulling out $300,000 in cash, and then decided that it was time to trade up again.

Their first step, of course, was to call Leo.

Epilogue

Bob and Jane's adventures continued into many of the other areas of commercial real estate, which included

- Office space
- Multifamily housing
- Industrial/warehouse
- Land development

- Apartment buildings
- Shopping malls

And they bought more residential property that they rented out: single-family homes, duplexes (two units), and fourplexes (four units). Ultimately, they gave up their regular jobs and devoted their entire time to managing their budding real estate empire. Soon they had fully paid off personal homes in both Marina Del Ray (California) and South Beach (Florida), as well as a condo in Vail (Colorado).

They both retired in their forties.

Questions Successful Investors Ask

I f you're new to real estate investing, you're bound to have lots of questions—dozens of them. However, just a few are likely to be the basic questions that all investors ask on their way to success. These are questions such as:

What's my time frame for becoming a success?
What if I don't have any money?
How do I set realistic goals?
What if my finances are in a shambles?
How do I know I have the qualities necessary to succeed?

These are reasonable questions to ask. After all, you don't want to dive into a pool until you've determined how deep the water is. Similarly, you shouldn't dive into real estate investing until you've plumbed the financial depths involved. Here are some answers to help you.

How Much Money Do I Need to Get Started?

As we saw in the last chapter, you don't need a whole lot. Of course, the amount depends on where you're starting. If you want to buy your first rental house and you're willing to move into it for a while (as Bob and Jane did) before you subsequently rent it out and resell it, then the very best financing in the world is available to you.

You can get a mortgage for as much as 100 percent of the purchase price. That means that you can get financing to cover the entire cost of the home and sometimes more to cover much of the closing costs. Your out-of-pocket expenses can be as little as zero. Where else can you get into an investment for so little? (In Chapter 10 we'll go into the details of financing.)

Of course, it's a different story if you buy a home with the express intention of using it as an investment rental. You'll need to put anywhere from a minimum of 10 to as much as 25 percent down plus closing costs. On a $200,000 home, that's about $20,000 to $50,000—a substantial sum of money. That's why buying to move in makes such good financial sense.

Should I Plan on Investing in Real Estate Full-Time?

In the beginning, it's usually a mistake to work full-time at investing in real estate. The reason is that you're unlikely to see much positive cash flow for the first few years. For most people, the best way to invest in property is usually on a part-time basis.

Don't expect to be flipping properties and getting rental income right away. As I said, it's unlikely that initially you'll get enough income to live on out of your properties. After a few years, when the properties have aged and values and rental rates have gone up, it's a different story. But for the first few years, it's better to think in terms of reinvesting income, rather than withdrawing it.

Be very wary of so-called real estate gurus who promise you tens of thousands of dollars of annual income from real estate from the moment you begin investing. If it is that easy, why aren't they making millions doing it themselves instead of selling get-rich-quick seminars on the subject? (By the way—in case you haven't already guessed—this is not a get-rich-quick book. Here we're talking about building your wealth in real estate the proven old-fashioned way—over time.)

All of this means that you need to have a steady full-time job for at least the first few years you are investing because your property isn't likely to yield enough steady income for you to live on. The most successful real estate investors I've known (myself included) buy property for the long term. If you go the long-term route, you won't have to worry as much about making occasional mistakes— because property values almost always go up with inflation and housing shortages, eventually you'll come out all right.

Most investors aim at just breaking even at first, and don't count on taking money out monthly. After a few years, however, when rental rates go up, they will probably be able to take out a strong, steady stream of income.

Try investing in real estate on the side. For a while at least, don't make it your primary objective. If you keep at it for enough years, you'll be able to retire early with a huge bounty to rely on.

Don't quit your day job! Make your goal part-time investing in real estate.

How Quickly Can I Get Money Out of My Real Estate Investments If I Need To?

In a period of 5 to 10 years, you might easily acquire a million dollars or more in equity in property. But you'll probably have very little cash in the bank. (This situation is spoken of as being "cash poor," a common condition for real estate investors.)

Being cash poor, however, is no longer the serious problem it was in the past. Today, with home equity loans and all types of refinancing possible, it's much easier to get cash out of your investment properties when you need it. All of which is to say that if you own a lot of property and have a sudden big personal expense, you'll probably have the means to cover it.

For example, let's say a big personal expense comes up, such as a sudden illness, a wedding, college education, or the need for a new car—anything that requires a lot of money. To get the money you need, you can *refi* (refinance) a property. (Alternatively, you could also sell a property, but that could take more time, and you would no longer have your investment.)

I always cringe when I hear people who purport to be financial advisors suggest that young couples put away a certain percentage of their income (usually into stocks and bonds, which these advisors often just happen to be selling) so that the couple will have the money to pay for their children's college education and their own retirement. (Their philosophy seems to be that you should live less well today by scrimping and saving so that you can live less well tomorrow!)

How much better it is to own a bunch of homes and other real estate, nearly paid off, that you can harvest for the money you need for these expenses when you need it. And you don't have to be scrimping and saving your entire life to pay for these investments—your tenants will handle that for you!

TIP

Your goal is to acquire properties in order to have the money you need for life's big expenses.

What's a Reasonable Time Frame for Success?

In other words, how long will it take you to make your fortune in real estate?

Of course, we've touched on this in many places. The answer is, figure on as much as 10 years or more, and 20 years is ideal.

Yes, you may be very lucky and come across a series of properties that you can flip, split (subdivide one property into two, thus doubling your money), or otherwise sell quickly for a big profit. But depending on that is like gambling on the lottery. It's great if it comes in, but don't count on it. Instead, rely on the slow and steady and sure.

Think of it in simple terms. As our couple, Jane and Bob, did in the first chapter, plan on buying one house every year or two for 20 years. At the end of that time, you'll own 10 to 20 houses. The first house will be roughly half paid off. (The return on equity from a mortgage is greatest in the last years and least in the first years. Thus, after paying on the mortgage for two-thirds of the time (20+ years), the house will be roughly only half paid off.) Furthermore, inflation and housing shortages are likely to have made that first house worth two to three times what you paid for it, no matter what you paid for it!

Chances are that by the end of that 20+-year period, you'll have much more than a million dollars in equity that you can convert to cash if you need to. In addition, you'll have positive cash flow as well. Remember, rental rates on those early properties will probably go up (because of inflation and housing shortages in many areas) just as prices do. You'll be renting those properties for two to three times the original rent, even though your mortgage payments will be roughly the same as when you started (assuming you haven't refinanced)!

All of which is to say that in addition to having a large net worth, you'll also have a large monthly income. This is the point at which you can retire from your regular job and live off your properties.

And remember, we're not talking about doing something difficult or arcane. We're talking about buying one property every year or two for 20 years. What could be simpler?

Of course, there may be obstacles. You could have a bad year and lose your job for a time. But even if that happens, while you might not be able to buy a new home that year, you'll have the homes you already own to fall back upon.

And, if you're older when you start, you may not have 20 years. You may only have 10 or 5 or even less. If that's the case, then I suggest you concentrate more on buying properties suitable for flipping. You'll be passing over many of the longer-term properties looking for those deep bargains that can more quickly line your pocket.

Of course, those who see the glass as always half empty will say that you could get sick or die, or the economy could nosedive. Yes, those things could happen. But they're going to happen whether or not you invest in real estate. So why not invest and hope for the best?

What Mindset Do I Need to Be a Successful Beginning Investor?

There is really only one requirement: you have to understand the difference between your business and your personal life.

When you are buying your first home for investment instead of pleasure, you will feel countless tugs, against your better judgment, to buy a property because it offers so many pleasing features. You may love the layout of the kitchen. The tile in the bathroom may be adorable. The backyard may be perfect for your family. The garage is ideal because it's big with lots of storage space—and there's a workbench!

All of these would be good reasons to select a home for your personal life, a home that would be most suited to your tastes, needs, and desires. However, when buying investment property, you need to put all that aside and let the reasoning portion of your mind take over. You need to be all business.

As we saw in the last chapter, the real questions to ask yourself are: Will this feature or that one be suitable for tenants? Is it easily replaced if it is damaged or destroyed? Will the feature make the house more or less salable in the future?

You have to put aside all personal feelings when you consider the property. You must be strictly business.

This also applies when it comes to money. When it's time to buy or sell a property, you must go for the very best deal possible. You can't let yourself be swayed by feeling sorry for the other party's situation. For example, tenants may tell you that they can't (or won't) pay their rent because they have so many other bills. You have to be strong enough to tell them, "The rent comes first," and demand immediate payment. (If you acquiesce to a tenant's problem, it then becomes your problem because you won't have the rental money with which to pay *your* bills.)

TRAP

Never make it personal—remember, it's business.

Similarly, when you are negotiating for the purchase or sale of a home, you may find that you're dealing with people who have all sorts of personal problems, from illness, to divorce, to bankruptcy. Your heart may go out to them. However, the way you help them is not by making their problem yours (by paying too much or selling for too little). It's by helping to remove a problem from them. For example, you can help people who are destined to lose their house to foreclosure by buying it from them, which will help them save at least some of their credit. If you want to go further and give them money to help them get back on their feet, I applaud you. However, be sure you understand your motivation. Getting someone's home out of foreclosure is business. Helping that person is charity. Both are admirable, but it's important not to confuse one with the other.

Your mindset must be that you're a businessperson, that you're involved in a business, and that your decisions are business decisions.

What Other Qualities Do I Need If I Am to Be Successful?

I have been asked if a successful real estate investor needs to have a mind that pays attention to detail. The answer is yes, certainly. But then again, it's hard to imagine any line of endeavor in which *lack* of attention to detail is an asset.

To be a successful real estate investor, you'll find that you need to keep track of market values, rental payments, and all sorts of numbers. A good ledger (or Palm Pilot) will help. But it's still up to you to remember the details.

I have also been asked if a person needs to be a "people person" to make a good real estate investor. Again, it's hard to imagine any line of work in which personal interactions aren't important. However, they can be less important in real estate investing than in other endeavors.

You don't need to "sell yourself" to purchase investment property or to be a landlord. Although a pleasing personality and a determination to deal fairly with people are great assets here and elsewhere in this business, many very successful real estate investors are actually reclusive. You almost never see them, and when you do, they don't have 10 words to say.

On the other hand, if you intend to sell a property on your own (for sale by owner, or FSBO), then it helps to be gregarious in nature. You'll be dealing directly with potential buyers, and if you have an ability to chat and make friends easily, it will help. Of course, you don't have to sell FSBO because you can always sell through an agent.

The Bottom Line

Thus, it turns out that you don't need a lot of money to get started. But you do need determination and the ability to separate your business from your personal life. You also need to understand that you're in it for the long term.

Opportunities in Foreclosures

Mention the word *foreclosure* and heads are sure to turn. To most people, the word is synonymous with *bargain*. Most people believe there's lots of money to be made in foreclosures.

And indeed there is, but not in all of them. Not all foreclosures are bargains. Some offer true profit opportunities, while others are nothing but money losers for all concerned. Some foreclosures are very much worth the time and money it takes to obtain them; others you'd be better off running away from.

In this chapter we're going to look at how to separate the wheat from the chaff. We're going to examine what makes a good foreclosure opportunity and where to find it. And we're also going to see what to avoid.

What Are Foreclosures?

As those in real estate know, a foreclosure involves a borrower, a lender, and a property. Typically, to buy a property, a person will borrow money from a lender in the form of a mortgage (or trust deed, depending on the state). If the borrower makes the payments, then normally there's no problem. If, however, the borrower can't make the payments, then the lender's recourse is to take the property away from the borrower. This is called foreclosure. The lender then typically sells the property in an attempt to recoup the money it had loaned.

There are three stages to the foreclosure process:

1. **Preforeclosure.** The borrower isn't making payments. The lender sends letters, calls, e-mails, and makes other attempts to get the borrower to catch up. When nothing works, the lender files a "notice of default" with the country recorder and sends the borrower a copy. This officially lets the borrower know that he or she is in default on the mortgage and normally gives the borrower a statutorily allowed amount of time to catch up with all interest and penalties. (The time varies from state to state, but is typically from a few months to as long as a year.) The borrower still owns the property.

2. **Auction.** Time's up. The lender now goes to court to force a foreclosure sale, which takes place on the courthouse steps (in states such as Florida where judicial foreclosure is the rule), or instructs a trustee to sell the property on the courthouse steps in trust deed states (such as California). At the auction, the lender normally bids the full amount of its loan. Anyone else, of course, can bid, and the highest legitimate bid wins.

TIP

A traditional mortgage is between a lender and a borrower and can be foreclosed only judicially—through court action. A "deed of trust" involves not only the borrower and the lender, but also a trustee who actually holds title; it can be foreclosed far more quickly and without going to court. Trust deeds are increasingly becoming the loan instrument of choice for lenders and are widely used on both coasts.

3. **Lender owned.** Assuming that the lender wins at the auction, it now owns the property. In the trade these properties are called "REOs" (real estate owned). The lender will now usually do what's necessary to fix up the property, then typically lists it for sale with an agent.

You can buy the property at any of the stages. In stage 1, you can buy the property from the borrower. In stage 2, you can buy it at public auction. In stage 3, you can buy it from the lender. However, as we'll see, just because you can buy it doesn't mean you should.

How Do You Find Out about Foreclosures?

In the old days (meaning before the Internet), finding out about foreclosures in any of the stages was fairly difficult. You'd have to search courthouse records for notices of default to learn about preforeclosures and legal notices in newspapers to learn about auctions. (Or subscribe to a local newspaper that did this for you, often for hundreds of dollars a month.) And you'd typically have to call on lenders directly to find out about their REOs.

Today, it's much easier. Internet sites such as www.foreclosure. com and www.realtytrac.com, as well as many others, provide listings of properties in all three stages. You simply go to the site and typically pay a nominal fee to join the service; then you too can learn about foreclosures in your area.

The Subprime Mortgage Meltdown

At any given time, there are hundreds of thousands of foreclosures on the market. During hard times, however, such as during the subprime mortgage meltdown, there are millions.

Mainly during the period between 2003 and 2006, lenders offered mortgages to subprime borrowers who very often couldn't afford them. The mortgages had very low introductory interest rates, which made the initial payments artificially low. However, after two or three years, these mortgages reset to much higher interest rates, resulting in much higher payments. When the borrowers couldn't make the new payments, they tried to resell. However, by then the market had taken a nosedive, and they couldn't find buyers. So they tried to refinance. But because the market had fallen, the borrowers often did not have enough equity in the property to warrant a refinanced mortgage. Besides, many of the lenders had decided to no longer offer subprime mortgages—so the borrowers couldn't refinance. Hence, they were forced into foreclosure.

You can find these subprimes in various stages of foreclosure on the Web sites noted earlier.

Buying a Home in Preforeclosure

Remember that a home that is in preforeclosure is still owned by the borrower. Thus, you must negotiate directly.

Often the borrower has tried unsuccessfully to sell the property, both using an agent and as a FSBO (for sale by owner). By the time you arrive on the scene, the borrower is very likely to be frustrated, angry, scared, and uncooperative. Thus, you have quite a few hurdles to leap before you can successfully make a deal for the property.

Furthermore, during preforeclosure, borrowers usually do not make any payments. (They are so far behind that they figure it's hopeless, so why throw good money after bad?) That means that in order to satisfy the lender, you'll have to pay off not only all the principal owed, but also any accrued interest and penalties.

As we saw in Chapter 1, with subprime mortgages, frequently a monthly payment less than the interest meant that interest that was not paid was added to the mortgage, meaning that the amount due could be much larger than the amount originally borrowed.

And when you add in a market in which prices are falling, often the result is that the borrower owes more than the property is worth. He or she is "upside down." (Which is another reason the borrower couldn't resell.)

The only way that you can profitably acquire a property in this situation is if the lender is willing to accept less than the amount it is owed—a "short sale." Getting the lender to do this, however, can be very tricky.

TRAP

The big problem is that many preforeclosure borrowers will refuse to let you negotiate with the lender for a short sale and/or will demand an unrealistic amount of money from you for releasing the property. In either of these cases, you simply have to realize that this not an opportunity, and walk away.

Contacting the Borrower

Personal contact is best. Once a notice of default has been filed, everyone knows about the preforeclosure and is contacting the borrowers. Lenders that want the borrowers to refinance (whether or not they are able to do so), agents that want listings, investors (such as yourself) that are looking for bargains, and "fixers" claiming that they can save the borrowers' credit (they usually can't) typically barrage the borrowers with letters, phone calls, and e-mails.

Very, very few, however, make a personal appearance. Therefore, to get the inside track on the competition, it's usually to your advantage to show up and talk to the borrowers personally.

Before doing this, however, you'll want to get all your ducks in a row. You'll want to find out exactly how much is owed on the property (which you can often learn from the foreclosure Web sites) and what the market value of the property actually is (which you can learn for free by doing a CMA—comparative market analysis—gleaning information on recent sales through Web sites such as www.zillow.com). You'll also want to learn about the neighborhood, schools, crime rates, and so on—all those things that are necessary parameters for investing, as described in Chapter 1.

Then, as noted, you'll need to negotiate a deal with the seller . . . and often with the lender.

Dangers of Dealing Direct

There are many tricks and traps in buying while a person is in default. For example, have your attorney find out if the borrower has filed for bankruptcy. (Many people who are facing foreclosure do.) If the borrower has filed, he or she may not be able to sell you the property without court approval. The borrower/seller may not know this, or may forget to mention it when you're negotiating a purchase.

Also, in many states there are laws protecting sellers/borrowers who are in default from being preyed upon by unscrupulous speculators looking to rob them of their home equity. (Remember, you're an investor who is trying to help, not hurt, the person in preforeclosure. If the person actually has equity, you're willing to pay for it.) For example, if the borrower sells to you while in default, he or she may have a redemption period that could be as long as a year or more. During that time, you might be prohibited from renting out or reselling the property. Be sure to check with a good agent and/or attorney in your area to see what rules apply.

What You Have to Offer

It's important to remember that when you come calling on a pre-foreclosure, you aren't coming hat in hand. You're bringing gifts.

In most cases, at a minimum, you may be able to at least partially save the borrowers' credit. The information that they are late on payments and in default will undoubtedly already have been sent to credit bureaus. Little to nothing can be done about that.

But if you take over the property and pay off the mortgage, so that the borrowers avoid foreclosure, that's a big thing. Not having a foreclosure on their record can mean that within a year or two, the borrowers can apply for new credit, and perhaps even get another mortgage to buy another house.

Additionally, should the borrowers have equity, you can offer to buy that equity, or at least some of it, from them. By refinancing as well as putting in some of your cash, you may be able to bail them out

Finally, you can offer hope. Most borrowers who are in default feel helpless and believe that the situation is hopeless. You can offer to take the pain away. You'll make the foreclosure disappear, and they can then move on with their lives. Again, this is no small thing.

Negotiating with a Lender

We've touched on it, but it's important to understand that in order to pull off a successful purchase of a preforeclosure, you'll proba-bly need to get a lender to agree to a "short sale." That means the lender will accept less than it's owed, just to make a deal.

In normal financial times, few lenders will do this. However, today when lenders have hundreds of foreclosures coming in, they tend to be more willing. Often the biggest problem is getting to the right person in the lender's office and then getting that person to make a decision. With hundreds and hundreds of foreclosures on every desk, sometimes just getting the person to focus on your deal can be the real challenge.

Financing a Preforeclosure

Always keep in mind that you may be able to negotiate good financing with the existing lender, even when there's a short sale involved. Talk to the lender. It may be willing to let you assume the existing mortgage, or even give you a new and higher one, if you agree to pay the current interest rate.

Remember, however, that an owner who is in default on a mortgage generally knows that it is usually still possible for him or her to save the property by making up the back payments, penalties, and interest. (In the final stages of foreclosure, the only way to save the property may be to refinance and pay off the defaulted mortgage.) Hence, that owner is likely to want to negotiate some money from you for the real or imagined equity.

Unless you can use the existing lender, you will need to get new financing (get a new loan and pay off the existing defaulted mortgage). You do this the same way you would if you were purchasing any other property. Be sure you're preapproved (have applied for a mortgage, have submitted at a minimum a credit report, and have received a lender's preapproval). Contact a mortgage broker either in the physical world or online. Find out what a lender will give you on the property. Get a sales agreement from the borrower. Get a new loan and pay off the old defaulted one. But do it with an escrow and title insurance to be sure that you end up with an insured title to the property.

Keep in mind that with a preforeclosure, there is a timeline running, and there are deadlines. It takes time to get new financing—be sure you have it.

Lenders are in the business of making loans, not taking back property through foreclosure. They will almost always allow a borrower ample opportunity to make good on missed payments. Today, lenders are often required by the government to offer a payback plan designed to fit the borrower's needs and problems. Rarely will a lender begin foreclosure until the borrower is at least two to three months in arrears. And sometimes the lender will halt the process temporarily if it looks like the borrower can be bailed out (with your help).

Buying a Home at an Auction

Another option is to buy a property in foreclosure when the court or the trustee sells it to the highest bidder at a public auction (often quite literally held on the courthouse steps). The time and date of the sale are advertised in a legal paper. And some Internet sites, such as those mentioned earlier, run that information.

However, unless you're a very experienced investor, I suggest that you *do not* attempt to buy a foreclosed property at this stage. To my mind, the dangers far outweigh the opportunities.

For example, you may not know how much the total liens on the property actually amount to. There could be more than one mortgage on it, and the holders of other, higher mortgages may not be at the auction. There could be government liens on the property. There could be other hidden liens from creditors.

As a result, you could buy the property by paying off the mortgage that was foreclosing, only to later discover that what you thought was seller's equity was actually covered by other liens. The owner's equity and your profit could evaporate into nothing.

TIP

Savvy investors will conduct thorough lien searches through title insurance companies before bidding at a public foreclosure auction. They'll also secure title insurance.

In addition, the investors who bid at foreclosure auctions are often a close-knit group. I've seen auctions where they force new bidders out by first bidding high, then rolling back their bids after the newcomer has dropped out. It's a tricky process and not for the faint of heart or the innocent.

If you're determined to bid at a foreclosure auction, get an agent who's done it many times before to guide you. And also be sure that your attorney checks out the purchase, the property, and the title.

TRAP

Beware of an "equity of redemption." In most states, the original borrower who is losing a property to a foreclosure auction has it, and it allows him or her to reclaim title even after a foreclosure sale. You may be prohibited from reselling, renting, or remodeling the property because of this. Check with a good attorney in your area before you buy.

Buying a Foreclosure from a Lender

When a lender obtains a property through foreclosure, it becomes an REO. REOs are typically owned by banks and mortgage bankers. [When large secondary lenders such as Fannie Mae and Freddie Mac, or government insurers such as the Department of Housing and Urban Development (HUD), or guarantors such as the Veterans Administration (VA) take back real estate through foreclosure, it's generally known as a "repo." See the end of this chapter for more information on these.]

Lenders hate REOs. The reason is simple: their whole purpose is to collect interest on money that they lend. Having to take property through foreclosure indicates a failure of their lending practices.

Furthermore, the federal government often requires lenders to maintain additional reserves when they have REOs (and to a lesser extent when they have loans that are in default) in case the ultimate disposition of the property results in a loss. These reserves are a big drain on a lender's capital. Which makes lenders hate REOs even more.

As a result, lenders are usually very anxious to get rid of these properties. However, they also want to get top dollar for them to avoid recording a loss. That's often a problem not only because of a poor market, but also because of the poor condition of most REOs.

Properties in Poor Condition

Very often, REOs are run-down, derelict properties. After all, why should an owner bother to keep up the property when he or she is about to lose it to foreclosure? Furthermore, after the former borrowers have moved out, vandals may sometimes have broken the windows, knocked holes in the walls, and set fires. Often, it's hard for the lender to protect the properties adequately during the preforeclosure stage. Thus, REOs often come to the lender in very bad shape.

But remember, the lender wants top dollar. So, typically the lender will spend the money necessary to make the REO presentable for sale. Then the lender will usually list the property at market price. As a result, often there's no bargain here for you (although the lender will sometimes offer more favorable terms, such as a smaller down payment or smaller monthly payments).

If, however, you can get to the lender before it fixes up the REO, then you may be able to swing a better deal. As with most things in life, timing is everything.

Buying an REO

Like preforeclosures and auctions, lender-owned properties are typically listed on foreclosure Web sites. Often there's one real estate office in an area that specializes in them (one for each lender). Find those offices and you've found your REOs.

The real opportunity with REOs, however, is usually to buy them as soon after the foreclosure auction as possible, before the lender has spent the money to fix them up. To do that, you'll need to contact the officer of the lender who handles them. It's another case of going direct.

Unfortunately, as suggested earlier, you'll have to make contact with each lender individually. (Look for lenders who have listed a lot of REOs with agents. Chances are they'll also have a lot that they have taken back but haven't yet listed.)

Once you find a property you're interested in, make an offer directly to the lender, often through an agent. My suggestion is that in addition to the usual contingencies found in any offer (such as financing, inspections, disclosures, and so forth), you also consider asking for allowances. This is particularly true before the lender has cleaned up the property.

Ask for a cleanup/fix-up allowance, and make it big enough to cover the job. (Reread Bob and Jane's bid on the Lexington Drive property in Chapter 1.)

You also may want to ask the lender to carry the financing for you. But, quite frankly, you're likely to get a better deal if you arrange your own outside financing. The reason, quite simply, is that most lenders simply want to be done with the property. They don't want any strings that could possibly land it back in their laps again.

Of course, as always in real estate, when you're dealing with a lender, remember that everything is negotiable. It all depends on how desperate the lender is to get rid of the particular property and how much money the lender has in it. It often comes down to how good a negotiator you are. [I suggest you look at my *Tips and Traps When Negotiating Real Estate* (McGraw-Hill).]

Dangers of Buying an REO

One of the biggest problems with buying an REO is that you're unlikely to get meaningful disclosures. After all, the lender doesn't really know much about the problems, so what can it disclose? (Unlike an occupant seller, who is likely to know everything about a property.)

The roof may leak, the structure may be unsound, the heater/air conditioner may be broken, and so on. There's probably nobody around to tell you.

So you need to conduct a good inspection. Hire a good inspector . . . or two. But keep in mind that property inspectors usually report on only what they can see. If a cracked floor is covered by a carpet, or if structural damage is contained within a wall, or if there's mold hidden under the floorboards, they may not find it. A brief inspection may not turn up real problems in an REO.

Another concern is renters or former owners. They could still be occupying the property. If they are, you could have a devil of a time getting them out. (An "unlawful detainer" eviction action on your part might be necessary.)

To avoid this, I always demand that the lender see to it that the property is vacant before I take possession. The lenders have the lawyers to deal with this.

Finally, be sure that the lender can give you clear title and title insurance. If the property is locked up in litigation, probate, bankruptcy, or some other problem, consider just passing.

TIP

REOs usually offer the cleanest foreclosure deals. On the other hand, they seldom offer the best bargains.

Check Out Government Repos

As noted earlier, when the government backs a mortgage, after foreclosure, it usually takes over ownership of the property—now called a "repo." Today the government owns a tremendous number of repos, almost all of them houses. It is always trying to sell these properties. You can sometimes take advantage of these sales to get into a property at a bargain price.

Here are some of the more popular government repo programs and how to acquire the properties.

HUD Repos

The Department of Housing and Urban Development takes back one- to four-unit residential properties mainly through its Federal Housing Administration (FHA) program. The FHA insures lenders who make loans. When a borrower defaults, the FHA makes good on the loan to the lender, and it takes the property back. At any given time, it may have tens of thousands of repoed homes for sale across the country. You can check to see if there are any HUD homes in your area on the Internet at www.hud.gov.

Most HUD repos are going to be in the moderate to low price range. Additionally, these homes may not be in the best condition. HUD usually does not fix up these properties. That means that they may be in anywhere from average to really bad shape. Don't be surprised at the terrible condition in which you may find a HUD home. Remember that the former owner lost the property to foreclosure, and therefore had little incentive to keep it up. Additionally, there may have been vandalism since that time.

Making an Offer

HUD properties are usually listed with local agents, usually on their Web sites. You must make your offer through an agent who represents HUD. Once you locate a home that you're interested in, contact the referred agent and go see the property. The agent can arrange to have you walk through it. You'll also make your offer directly through the agent. You can find a list of agents handling HUD properties in your area at www.hud.gov/homes/.

Pricing

HUD tries to sell its homes at fair market price. However, sometimes this price is difficult to determine because of the run-down condition of the properties. Occasionally, particularly if you are sharp at knowing property values, you can find some real bargains here! (Check into Chapter 8 for tips on how to scout out run-down properties.)

Financing

HUD usually doesn't make loans directly, but it does work with lenders in a variety of programs. You may be able to get in with virtually nothing down, as long as you intend to occupy the home. If you're buying it as an investment, HUD will usually want at least 10 percent down. In other words, your financing needs are going to be similar to those for any investment property. (Look at Chapter 10 for tips on getting investment loans.) HUD often looks with extra favor on buyers who submit offers that are a cash-out to HUD. In other words, you get your own outside financing.

Owner-Occupants

Like many government programs, HUD aims to sell its homes to those who will occupy them. Read *not* to investors. Thus, in the "initial offer period," HUD looks at offers from people who intend to occupy the homes that are for sale through the HUD program. If you're looking for a house to both live in and invest in, this can be the perfect choice for you.

However, if no owner-occupants submit offers during the initial offer period, or if the home does not sell in that time frame, then investors can make offers that will be considered.

Does this mean that you as an investor have a chance at buying only the leftovers? Not really. Remember, most of these homes are not in great shape, so most owner-occupants are not eager to buy them. Furthermore, remember that HUD makes an effort to offer the homes at market price. For casual owner-occupant buyers who don't really know the market, it may not seem like there are any bargains here. As a result, very often these homes are sold to investors.

Fix-Up Allowance

If the home is in bad shape, HUD may offer a fix-up allowance. This can be in the form of either an additional price reduction or a special fix-up loan. However, in order to get this, you must be sure it's part of your purchase offer. Once you've made your offer and it's been accepted by HUD, it's too late to request a fix-up allowance.

Bonuses

HUD may also offer special incentives if it's particularly interested in moving a property. For owner-occupants, these incentives can include a moving allowance. For investors, they can include a bonus (price reduction) for closing the sale fast. If you have all your financing ducks in a row and can close within a week or two, you might realize a significant financial gain.

Professional Inspection

To avoid buying a pig in a poke, you'll want to have a professional inspection of the home. However, unlike conventional purchases, in which the professional inspection is normally conducted after you've signed a purchase agreement with the seller, when you work with HUD, you need to make your inspection beforehand. HUD doesn't like to tie up homes on contingencies that involve inspections.

As noted, at any given time, there are thousands of HUD homes for sale in virtually every state. If you're interested in working the repo market, you owe it to yourself to check out the HUD program.

VA Repos

The Veterans Administration has an extensive program of loan guarantees. Unlike HUD, which insures loans to lenders, the VA guarantees the performance of a loan to a lender. (Actually, it guarantees only a small percentage of the top of the loan.) If the borrower defaults, the VA pays off its guaranteed portion. However, rather than simply pay out cash, the VA, because it has determined that it is more profitable to do so, actually buys the property from the lender that forecloses and then resells it.

Initially, only those veterans who qualify (i.e., were on active duty during specific time periods) can get VA loans in order to buy a home. After the VA has foreclosed, however, it opens the sale to anyone, veteran or nonveteran, investor or owner-occupant.

Making an Offer

To purchase a VA home, you must go through a real estate agent who represents the VA's property management program, just as you would with the HUD program. Typically these agents will advertise in local newspapers.

You may also find most, but not all, of the properties listed on the VA's property management Web site. Unlike HUD, the VA does not maintain an Internet presence with a list of all the properties it has available for sale. It is up to the property management office to determine whether to link to the VA site and whether to list its homes on the Web. As of this writing, there were two Web links that were active for VA home sales. First, there is the VA's service provider: http://www.ocwen.com/reo/residential. You may also try the government site: http://www.homesales.gov/homesales/. To make an actual offer, you must go through an agent and use the proper forms. These include the following:

Offer to purchase/contract of sale (VA form 26–6705)
Credit statement (VA form 26–6705B)

Financing

The VA will handle some financing. However, it prefers to do this for owner-occupants. And it gives priority to buyers who come in with their own financing (cash to the VA). You will usually do better if you handle your own financing outside the VA.

Condition of the Property

Like homes in the HUD programs, many VA properties are in the same condition they were in when they were turned over after foreclosure. In the past, however, the VA has had an extensive program of refurbishing properties in order to get a higher market value. If you buy a refurbished home, don't expect to get any kind of bargain on the price. How the homes are handled is determined largely by the regional VA property management office.

Inspection

Again, you'll want to have a professional inspection so that you'll know what you're getting. However, as with HUD, you'll need to conduct the inspection during the offering period, not after your offer has been accepted. The agent who is handling the house can arrange for you and your inspector to see the property. Be sure you use a sharp pencil when you calculate how much the property is really worth.

The VA program has been in existence for over 50 years. I've been involved with it at different times and in different ways, and I have seen many owners obtain solid investment property through it.

Fannie Mae Properties

Fannie Mae and Freddie Mac (discussed next) are the main secondary lenders in the country. They underwrite most of the conventional (not government-insured or government-guaranteed) mortgages that are made. What this means is that when you get a mortgage from, say, XYZ lender, the lender then in effect sells your mortgage to Fannie Mae or Freddie Mac, from which it receives enough money to go out and make additional mortgages.

If, however, you fail to make your mortgage payments and fall into foreclosure, it's Fannie Mae or Freddie Mac (through whatever lender happens to be servicing the mortgage at the time) that may take the property back. Those agencies then have to get rid of it, similar to the way in which HUD or the VA must dispose of their properties.

This, again, can present an opportunity for investors.

Property Types

Fannie Mae underwrites all types of single-family homes, which include detached properties, condos, and town houses. Most of its inventory consists of fairly new homes, often in modest to even upscale neighborhoods. My own observation is that Fannie Mae properties tend to be a little classier than either HUD or VA homes.

Property Listings

Like HUD and the VA, Fannie Mae requires you to go through a local real estate agent. However, the agents are required to list all the homes on the local MLS, so there's no difficulty in gaining access. Any agent on the local board can show you the home, as well as make the offer for you. Your offer will then go to the listing agent, who will in turn present it to Fannie Mae.

You can also find a list of Fannie Mae homes at its Web site: fanniemae.com. Look for "Fannie Mae owned property search."

Making an Offer

The transaction is handled just as if you were dealing with any other conventional seller. Fannie Mae can accept, reject, or counter your offer. Indeed, you may go through several rounds of countering before the deal is finally done.

Unlike negotiations with either HUD or the VA, in presenting an offer to Fannie Mae, you can add contingencies and other conditions to your offer. You may ask to have a professional home inspection after the offer is accepted. You can also negotiate over terms, down payment, and financing. Fannie Mae will not, however, accept a contingency that requires the prior sale of a seller's current home.

You may use your own title insurance and escrow company. However, to have your offer accepted, you must usually be preapproved by a lender. That means that you've had your credit checked and your income and cash on deposit verified.

Condition of the Property

These are repos, which means that they may (or may not) be in poor condition. Sometimes Fannie Mae will fix up these properties in order to get a higher price. Other times, Fannie Mae will leave them in the condition in which it received them. In any event, all the homes are sold in "as-is" condition, meaning that the buyers must take the homes with whatever problems they have at the time of sale.

Financing

Fannie Mae does offer its own REO financing. However, it's typically not any better than you would get elsewhere. Furthermore, you may have a better chance of having your offer accepted if you come in with cash to Fannie Mae (that is, if you secure outside financing).

As with other government repo programs, to get a bargain, you must be on top of the market. You must be able to recognize true value where others miss it. Making a sharp offer can often net you an excellent deal.

Freddie Mac Properties

Like Fannie Mae, Freddie Mac offers single-family detached homes, condominium units, and town houses. However, Freddie Mac often cleans and fixes up its homes before offering them for sale. If you want to submit an offer on a home for which you propose doing the fix-up work yourself, chances are that Freddie Mac will still at least clean up the property to some extent before you buy it.

Through its HomeSteps program, Freddie Mac will offer homes to owner-occupants at competitive interest rates with 5 percent down payments and no mortgage insurance. It will also offset some of the title and escrow costs. These homes, however, are almost all competitively priced at market.

Freddie Mac homes are offered through a select group of lenders. To find out more about them, check out the Web site www.homesteps.com.

Other Government Repo Programs

There are many other government repo programs, including some from the IRS and local government authorities. Unfortunately, their URLs tend to change frequently. To find a current list of them, try using a search engine such as Google and entering the keywords "government repos."

Be aware, however, that there are hundreds of commercial sites, some of which appear to be official government sites. Know with whom you're dealing.

Many real estate gurus are fond of pointing out that a foreclosure is a crisis, and that in Chinese, the character for crisis means both "opportunity" and "danger." I have it on good authority that in terms of Chinese, this is nonsense and results from a misreading of Chinese characters.

On the other hand, in terms of foreclosure, it makes good sense. When you invest in a foreclosure, there is danger—danger that you'll pay too much, that you'll buy a property with hidden liens, that there are undisclosed defects, and so on.

On the other hand, there's also opportunity—opportunity to make a big profit.

Thus, the bottom line becomes: be careful.

Trading Your Way to a Real Estate Empire

Poker has become extremely popular of late—championship games are nationally televised to an audience of millions. In fact, poker is just about as popular as the national pastime of comparing home prices, in which most homeowners engage! All of which is fine because in many respects, investing in real estate is like playing a game of poker.

Here, I'm specifically talking about the "rake," which is what the casino or "house" takes from each pot for the privilege of letting you play. The amount of the rake varies from as much as 10 percent for small pots to less for larger pots.

I once talked with a poker master who told me that the rake was what secretly doomed poker players. He pointed out that if each player "invested" a set amount of money, given enough time, regardless of winners, losers, or skill levels, the house would eventually have all the money. It was inevitable; simply because of the house's "raking" in a small amount from every pot, every player would eventually be drained of all his or her capital.

While not as Draconian, something like this happens with taxes and real estate. Consider this: if every time you sold for a profit, the government (the "house," in poker vernacular) took a portion, after a lifetime of investing, you'd have far less. And the government would have far more.

Yet that's exactly what does happen. If you sell a rental house for a gain, you're taxed on that gain. If you sell an office building, an industrial site, a strip mall, a bare lot, or any other investment real estate for a gain, the government rakes in its share.

CAUTION
> This chapter presents some of the advantages of doing a Section 1031 tax-deferred exchange rather than a straight sale. It is not intended to advise you on doing such an exchange. Further, tax rules changes constantly, hence, you should not rely on this material. For tax advice, you should consult with a tax professional such as an accountant or tax attorney.

Let's take an example to make this perfectly clear. You sell an apartment building you've owned for over a year, and you have a gain of $500,000. The maximum federal capital gains rate currently is 15 percent. So you may owe $75,000 in capital gains taxes on the sale.

But that's just to the feds. You probably also owe capital gains taxes to your state. (State rates vary.) Let's say you owe another $25,000 in state capital gains taxes. That's a total of $100,000, or 20 percent of your capital.

Now you want to buy another property. Instead of $500,000, you've got only $400,000 to put into it. That means that you'll have to buy a smaller property. And you'll end up with a smaller equity.

Over time, as the government's rake continues with each new investment you sell, your real estate capital grows much more slowly—and you have much less of it.

Avoiding the Rake

My poker-master friend told me that the best way to win at poker is to find a place where there is no rake. "Find a game that has no house, be skillful, and you can make a fortune," he said.

The same applies to real estate. Find a way to avoid paying that capital gains tax, make skillful investments, and you'll build a much bigger real estate fortune faster.

But how do you avoid paying taxes on your real estate gains? Is there actually a way?

Yes, there is. You do a tax-deferred exchange of properties. In other words, you trade up.

Real estate that's held for the long term, generally meaning at least a year and one day, can be exchanged for other "like-kind" (discussed later) real estate, and the tax that would otherwise be due can be put off. If the exchange is done in accordance with the rules of tax code Section 1031, the tax on the gain on the old property is deferred and carried forward into the new property. There's no tax due on the exchange.

Each time you do this, because there's no tax to pay immediately, you have more capital to invest. You can buy bigger properties, and your equity in them is larger. You can grow your real estate fortune faster.

TIP

If you have gains from the recapture of depreciation, which are typically taxed at a higher rate, they are also deferred—another advantage of doing a 1031 exchange.

But, you may reasonably ask, what if you need to get your profit out to pay bills that you have? Don't you then have to sell for cash and pay taxes?

No, not necessarily. In that case, you refinance. You pull your money out by getting a loan. And the new mortgage normally has no tax consequences. (Typically, with the passage of time, your income from rents will increase to pay for the new, bigger mortgage.)

Thus you can grow your capital faster while still being able to get your cash out when you need it.

But, you may again reasonably ask, what happens when you want to retire and sell off your assets?

Why sell them for cash, ever? When you retire, you can have a property management firm handle the day-to-day operations of your rental property and receive a steady stream of income.

And when you die, let your heirs worry about it!

Actually, in 2007, the exclusion from the death tax is $2 million, and is going up to an unlimited amount in 2010. (After that, the exemption decreases, and Congress may determine the following year's amount.) Thus, it's likely that even your heirs won't have that much to worry about.

The Section 1031 tax-deferred exchange offers an enormous opportunity to grow your real estate wealth faster and better. It's one of the biggest advantages there is of investing in real property.

If you want to play a "what-if" game with your property involving a Section 1031 exchange vs. an outright sale, consider doing an online comparison. As of this writing, the Web site www.1031vest.com offers a "capital gains calculator." Just input the numbers and it will show you how much you might potentially save by doing the exchange.

What's Involved in a Section 1031 Tax-Deferred Exchange?

In Chapter 1, Bob and Jane did a tax-deferred exchange of a rental home for an office building. Reread that section if you're still not sure what a Section 1031 tax-deferred exchange is.

Here, we're going to take a somewhat more detailed look at some of the general dos and don'ts of Section 1031 tax-deferred exchanges.

Don't Try to Find a Simultaneous Exchange

Although the word *exchange* suggests that I give you something directly in exchange for what you give me, that's not what we're usually talking about. (Besides, that would be extremely difficult to arrange.) Here we're talking about a delayed exchange. (A simultaneous exchange would be one in which a property is exchanged for another property at the same time.)

A delayed exchange means that you sell your old property, and before the deal is concluded, you declare that you're doing an exchange. Your money is typically held away from you by a "qualified intermediary" (described later), and you have a certain time period in which to designate and then close on a new property. The rules for this are formalized.

What's important to understand is that the buyer of your old property need not be the seller of your new property. There can be two simple and separate deals. For you, however, there is technically an exchange.

Do Exchange for a "Like-Kind" Property

It's an apples-for-apples and oranges-for-oranges kind of thing. You can do a 1031 tax-deferred exchange provided that the properties being exchanged are being used for investment or held for productive use in a trade or business. In Chapter 1, we had a list of those types of properties that do not qualify as like kind. Here are some that normally do:

Like-Kind Properties for Real Estate

- House (rental)
- Condo (rental)
- Apartment building
- Office building
- Land (for development)
- Industrial building
- Office space
- Retail space
- Assisted-living facility
- Hotel or motel (There may be issues of personal property, discussed next.)
- And more

Most people believe that only real property (real estate) can be exchanged. That, however, is not necessarily so. In a "multiasset" exchange, personal property can be included. This would be the case when there is a trade of a hotel and personal property such as beds, furniture, TVs, linen, and so on are also part of the exchange.

Do Exchange for a Property of Equal or Greater Value

In order to defer all of your capital, you must trade up. That means that the new property must be of greater or at least of equal value. The same rule generally applies to mortgages.

If the new property you acquire has a value less than that of the old property you are giving up, the net difference between the two may be considered capital gain and taxed. If you end up with a smaller mortgage, the difference "forgiven" may be taxable.

Don't Take Boot

"Boot" means cash taken out of the exchange. For example, suppose you have $500,000 in capital gains. Instead of sticking all $500,000 into the new property, you take $150,000 in cash out of the exchange. That $150,000 becomes taxable immediately (in the year of the sale for a calendar-year taxpayer). You must put all the net proceeds from the old property into the replacement property in order to avoid paying a capital gains tax.

Furthermore, taking out boot can threaten the viability of the exchange. Although technically you can take out boot, pay the tax on it, and continue with the rest of the exchange, it becomes much more complicated. In order not to disqualify the exchange, all of the "safe haven" rules (those that the IRS requires for a Section 1031 exchange) must be scrupulously observed.

If you want to take boot out, be sure that you are working with an experienced expert in Section 1031 exchanges.

Do Watch the Timelines

The timelines are simple, but inflexible. Miss a deadline, and your tax-free exchange suddenly disappears and you've got a sale on which you probably owe a substantial capital gains tax.

There are two basic timelines in a delayed exchange. The first is that you have 45 days to identify your replacement property. That's from the time you sell your old property.

The second timeline is that you have 180 days to close the deal on your replacement property. Again, that's from the time you sell your old property (or the due date of your federal tax return for the year in which you do the exchange, whichever occurs first).

TRAP

It's important to understand that both of these timelines are triggered by the transfer of your old property. It's not that you first have 45 days to identify a property or properties and then have 180 days to close. The timelines run concurrently.

Do Identify the Replacement Property or Properties Carefully

It would seem to be easy to simply identify one replacement property and then close on it. However, because of the time limits, if for any reason you can't close in the time available, you might lose your exchange. Therefore, most investors try to identify multiple properties. This allows the investor to, so to speak, have a spare or two, just in case.

It's important to understand that you can indeed exchange multiple properties. You are not limited to exchanging one property for one other. You can exchange multiple properties for multiple other properties. However, there are strict rules for identifying the replacement properties.

There are three rules for identifying replacement properties for an exchange. The most commonly used is the "up to three rule." It says that you can identify up to three properties without regard to their value.

Then there is the 200 percent rule. Here, you can identify any number of properties, but the combined value of all of them cannot exceed double the value of the old property you are giving up.

Finally, there's the 95 percent rule. Again, there are no limits on the number of properties you can identify. However, you are required to acquire 95 percent of the aggregate fair market value of 95 percent of all the identified properties.

You can use any of the three rules.

Don't Cross the Border

Most people understand that a Section 1031 exchange works for properties here in the United States. However, many investors mistakenly believe that it also works for a intercountry exchange. In other words, they believe that you can exchange a property here in the United States for one in Mexico or some other country.

Not so. You can do a Section 1031 exchange for properties here in the United States. Or you can do one for properties wholly outside the United States. But you can't do an exchange across the American border. For example, you can't do a Section 1031 exchange of an American property for a property in Canada.

Do Use a Qualified Intermediary

A qualified intermediary is a party who helps the exchange avoid creating boot by contaminating funds. Remember, any time there's boot, it may become taxable. Thus, what do you do with your funds after your old property closes, but before you can close on your replacement property? Any time you, as the investor in the exchange, take control of those funds, you may have, even inadvertently, created taxable boot.

Thus, a qualified intermediary should handle the funds and facilitate the exchange.

What does "qualified" mean? The biggest qualification of the intermediary is that he/she/it is independent of the taxpayer. A qualified intermediary can be virtually anyone *except* someone who has a close business or financial relationship with the taxpayer. People who are *dis*qualified usually include blood relatives, the agent, the attorney, the lender, and the accountant. (Some 1031 specialists suggest that if you haven't done any deals with your agent in the previous two years, that person may qualify—check with a good tax attorney.)

Once you have a qualified intermediary, that party can facilitate the exchange, including holding funds and directing the transfer of title. (There are online sites that provide 1031 intermediary services such as 1031vest.com.)

Don't Limit Yourself to a Delayed Exchange

While the previous discussion was primarily for a delayed exchange, there are other types of exchanges as well. For example, there's a "reverse exchange."

In a reverse exchange, you acquire your replacement property before selling your old property. Of course, to avoid receiving boot or nullifying the exchange, you cannot take title to that replacement property until you sell your old property. Thus, the replacement property is typically "parked" with a neutral third party, also called an exchange accommodation titleholder (EAT). You can park the new property for up to a maximum of 180 days.

There is also a "build-to-suit" exchange. Here, you are allowed to construct (or modify) a new building on the replacement property using the proceeds from the sale of the old property. Again, the construction has a maximum time limit of 180 days for completion, and again an independent third party has to hold title during that construction phase.

What it's important to gather from this chapter is that it's often a mistake to simply sell investment property outright, because of the tax consequences. Doing so means that you'll end up owing taxes on your gain and giving up a significant part of your capital (letting the government rake it in).

A Section 1031 exchange provides the opportunity for you to defer paying capital gains taxes, at least for the moment. And it allows you to use all of your capital to purchase your next property.

The Section 1031 exchange is like a ladder boosting you to ever higher property investments. Just make sure you get professional assistance with your exchange.

Fortunes in Flipping

Whenever I hear the term *flipping*, I'm always reminded of a fish out of water. However, flipping has nothing to do with fishing. Rather, it's a term that is used to refer to the rapid turnover of a property, or flipping ownership. It means selling a property shortly after buying it. Indeed, it can mean never actually taking title to the property, but instead making a profit by tying it up and then quickly dumping it.

Flipping is fashionable mainly when there is a hot market. When properties are jumping in value at rates of 10, 15, or sometimes 25 percent a year or more, it's fairly easy to lock in a price and then resell for a higher price in very short order.

For example, you may buy a house for $150,000 and, in a hot market, be able to quickly resell it for $175,000. If you're careful about how you do this and avoid most of the transaction costs, you can pocket a quick $25,000. In some cases, of course, the profit can be substantially more.

On the other hand, in a more normal market with perhaps 5 percent price appreciation annually, or in a falling market, flipping is more difficult. Here it's much harder to find a property whose price will go up so rapidly that a flip is justified. But for savvy investors who spend time looking, bargain-priced properties are still available, and flipping these does make sense.

How Do You Flip Properties?

To flip real estate successfully, you need to follow certain guidelines. These guidelines are not hard and fast, but if you break them, you could suffer a loss.

Rule 1: Buy low. The only ways you can gainfully flip a property are to pay less than market price for it or to buy it at market price and wait for its value to rise. You cannot make money by paying over market for properties or buying ones that do not quickly go up in value.

Rule 2: Lock in the low price. If you lock in a price, you can resell for a higher price. If you don't lock in a price, then the seller can easily sell to the next person and make the profit himself or herself.

Rule 3: Have your rebuyer ready. A rebuyer is the person who buys the property from you. Since time is of the essence in these deals, you usually don't have time to lock up a property and *then* go out looking for a rebuyer. You must have one who is ready to act.

And that's how it's done. No, not really, as we'll quickly see. But those three rules form the basics. Of course, there is one other consideration, and that's keeping yourself out of trouble while you're flipping. You do this through full disclosure. You let all parties know what's happening. That way, there's less chance that someone will come back later on and say that he or she didn't know what was going on and, hence, was cheated.

Can I Flip a New Home?

This happens only when the market is hot and there are shortages of homes. Then people wait in long lines to buy new homes, and many of them are hoping to flip the property. If there are 20 new homes being built and the demand is for 500 (as was the case in some areas in recent years), that means that 480 people are not going to get a new home. If you're one of the lucky 20, you can quickly sell to one of the unlucky others.

Can I Flip a Resale?

Savvy investors are always on the lookout for properties that are for sale at or below market. If they find them, they tie them up and then quickly resell them. Sometimes the sales are from foreclosures, REOs, or probates, or just from sellers who want out quickly and are willing to take less.

How Do I Flip a Property?

It's really not that hard to do. The key is to lock in the price. Once you locate a property that's selling for below market, you present an offer that ties up the seller. If the seller accepts, you have a period of time in which to resell. Depending on how your offer was structured, your time period can be anywhere from a minimum of about 30 days to a maximum of about six months.

TIP

The most advantageous way to handle a flip often is never to take title yourself. The mechanics of doing that can be fairly complex. However, the advantage is that you don't obtain a mortgage, so you don't need to qualify or pay mortgage costs or, sometimes, even closing costs.

You then bring in your rebuyer (the one who actually purchases the property), who concludes the sale with the original seller. The money transfer is all done in escrow. The new buyer gets a mortgage and puts up a cash down payment in the usual fashion. A portion of the purchase price goes to cash out the original seller. And you get the difference, usually in cash, but sometimes in the form of a second mortgage, for yourself.

There are two methods commonly used to accomplish this: assignment and options. The option is the easier to understand.

What Is an Option?

Real estate options are not much different from stock options. For the buyer, they are an opportunity (but not a requirement) to purchase for a set price by some future date. For the seller, they are a commitment to sell, usually for a set price, by a set date.

The basics of an option are fairly straightforward. First, you locate the property and make an option offer. If the sellers accept, you next give them option money (perhaps $100 at a minimum), and they in exchange give you the right to purchase the property, usually at a fixed price, for up to a certain amount of time, typically no more than six months or a year (although any time length is possible).

Next, you find a rebuyer, someone who will purchase the property from you at a higher price. This is the person whom you, hopefully, have ready to go.

Finally, you exercise the option at the low fixed price agreed to by the seller, and then sell to the rebuyer at the new higher price, keeping the difference, which is your profit. In actual practice, all of these moves are made simultaneously, and the seller pays the normal seller's closing costs and the rebuyer pays the normal buyer's closing costs, with very few transaction costs left for you to pay.

And it really is that almost that simple. The key, of course, is finding the right-priced property, the right seller, and the right rebuyer.

TIP

In an option, you the buyer are not committed to purchase. It's at your discretion. The seller, however, is committed to sell, usually at a fixed price. He or she must go through with the transaction if you exercise your option.

The right property is one that either is undervalued or is located in an area where prices are accelerating. The right seller is usually someone who wants to get out and is strapped for immediate cash.

Remember, in order to get an option, you pay the seller some money. It can be any amount, but it has to be enough to persuade him or her to give you an option. A typical amount might be between $100 and $5,000, depending on the value of the property.

The biggest problem with an option is the time factor. The term of the option is negotiable. Usually options run from 30 days to six months, but they can be for virtually any length of time. The trouble is that sellers usually want out quickly, and a seller who is willing to give you an option for more than 60 days is unlikely to be willing to also give you a good price.

In the past, options in real estate were used primarily for properties other than residential. They were used to buy land, commercial or industrial buildings, farms, and so on. They were used to allow the buyer time to obtain difficult financing, for example, or to secure a change in zoning, or for some other similar reason.

Recently, however, they have been increasingly used in residential real estate as part of a flipping strategy. In these cases, the time frame is typically very short, generally less than three months, and the amount of option money given to the seller is likewise usually small, typically under $5,000.

TIP

Remember, the key to flipping (using the option) is to have a rebuyer waiting and ready to go. If you have that rebuyer ready, you can handle a transaction easily in 60 days. Indeed, you can handle it in 30 days, or perhaps even less. But if you have to go out and find a rebuyer once you have the option, the time factor reduces the likelihood of your success in the deal.

How Do I Handle the Paperwork for an Option?

You can get an option document at most stationery stores or legal supply houses. This is what the seller will sign to give you the option. However, before attempting to use it, you should take it to an attorney, who will rewrite portions of it to suit your specific deal.

When it comes time to exercise the option, you simply open an escrow account as if you were going to buy the property. However, your rebuyer does all the qualifying for the mortgage and puts up the down payment and all the normal closing costs.

When the deal is ready to close, your option is exercised (or assigned to the rebuyer). For a moment you may own the property, but then it is transferred to the rebuyer. It is all handled in escrow.

NOTE

While an option is not complicated, there is plenty of room to make a mistake. Therefore, at the very least, the first time you use it, you should have someone experienced, such as a good agent or attorney, lead you through it. Yes, that will cost you more, but in the long run it can save you a lot of headaches (and possibly money).

TIP

It's important that you disclose to the rebuyer the amount that you are actually paying for the property. This avoids hard feelings and helps protect you from that rebuyer coming back later and saying that he or she was cheated. It's also a good idea to let the seller know what you're doing, although when you have a valid option, it's really none of the seller's business what you do with the property after you exercise your option.

What about an Assignment?

Another way to tie up the property without buying it is to use an assignment of purchase. In this type of arrangement, you make an offer to purchase, usually for cash. However, when you make your offer, you state that the buyer is your name or assigns. What this means is that either you can buy the property or someone else to whom you have assigned the contract can buy the property.

Later on, you have your rebuyer step in, and you assign the purchase contract to him or her. Your rebuyer actually gets the financing and makes the purchase. And you pocket the difference between what you paid for the property and the higher price that the rebuyer pays.

Getting a seller to agree to an assignment, however, can be tricky. Some sellers won't go along with an "or assigns" sales contract. The reason is that they don't know who will eventually purchase the property. They are afraid that you might not be able to get the mortgage you need and want a back door out, or that you're planning to sell your contract to someone else (which is, in fact, the case!) who may not qualify for a mortgage. In order to calm the seller's fears, you may need to put up a bigger deposit or avoid putting many escape clauses into the contract, which can increase your risks.

Unlike an option, the ability to assign the contract runs only as long as the purchase contract is in effect, typically 30 to 45 days. That means that you've got to find a buyer and conclude the other end of the deal very quickly.

Hopefully you have done your homework and have a rebuyer waiting in the wings. This person picks up the assignment and actually moves forward with the purchase of the property. Again, you never actually make the purchase. The transaction is basically handled in escrow. At the end of the deal, you get your money out, typically in cash. The advantages of assignment are the following:

- You don't need to put in your own cash. You have to put up only the original deposit when you buy the property from the seller, and you get this deposit back from your rebuyer.
- You can expect to get your profit out within 30 to 45 days.
- You don't have to qualify for or obtain a mortgage.

Problems with Assignments

Of course, it's not all a bed of roses. There are risks. You actually do commit to purchasing the property. To protect yourself from having to complete the purchase in case you can't find a rebuyer (or in case your rebuyer falls through), you'll want escape clauses. But escape clauses weaken your offer and lessen your chances of getting it accepted. So to make the deal, you may not be able to include many (or any) such clauses and have to take a big risk.

Assignments have been used in real estate for a long time. However, as noted earlier, you need to include lots of escape clauses in the deal in case you can't find a buyer in the short amount of time that you have, or in case that buyer, for some reason, can't complete the purchase.

Escape Clause? What's That?

An escape clause is a provision that lets you back out of the deal gracefully (without penalty). Typically, it says that the sale and purchase are "subject to" or "contingent upon" something. If that something happens, you can, without financial harm, back out of the deal. In modern transactions, there are three widely accepted escape clauses that most sellers will agree to without blinking an eye:

Disclosure contingency. You must approve the seller's disclosures. If you don't approve them, there's no deal. But the time limit here is very short. In California, for example, it is statutorily three days. And if the sellers disclose nothing wrong, it's awkward to disapprove the deal.

Professional inspection contingency. You get to approve a professional inspector's report. If you don't approve it, there's no deal. Usually you have 14 days to get the report and then either approve or disapprove it, and if there's nothing wrong with the property, it's hard to disapprove the report.

Finance contingency. You have written into the contract that the deal is contingent upon your getting financing. No financing, no deal, and you're out without penalty. This usually runs for 30 days, but you must reasonably look for financing.

The language for these contingencies must be appropriate for your state and locale. Therefore, at least until you learn how it's done, you need to have a good agent or attorney write them in for you.

NOTE

The problem with these contingencies is that they probably don't offer you enough protection if you're making an assignment. They are for short periods of time, and they may not apply in your case. For example, in order to get the deal at a cut-rate price, you may have to offer the seller cash. In a cash sale, you don't have the protection of a finance contingency.

You might rely on the disclosure or the professional inspection contingency, but those usually run out after 14 days max. (And if there's nothing untoward about the property, you would be hard pressed to exercise them.) Once they run out, you either agree to move forward without their protection or back out of the deal.

If you agree to move forward and something adverse happens (your rebuyer backs out), you're stuck with the house!

As a result, most investors who are flipping using an assignment want to add other contingencies. These contingencies are easy to add, but not easy to get accepted by the seller.

You can make the sale contingent on anything: your uncle's dying and giving you an inheritance, your great aunt's coming from Greece to approve the deal, sunspots, anything at all. However, any contingency you add that is not reasonable (such as the three just mentioned) is likely to be considered frivolous by the seller and a reason not to sell to you. Thus, the more escape clauses you include, the less likely you are to get the seller to sign. And the fewer escape clauses you include, the greater your risk in case you can't close the deal.

Some investors feel that there may be another way to help limit your liability in case you can't make the deal. Most modern purchase agreements include a liquidated-damages clause. If you sign this (and the seller does too), then the total amount of damages that you are likely to have to pay in the event that you don't (or can't) make the deal is usually limited to your deposit. If you put up only $1,000 for a deposit, you don't have a great deal at risk.

However, it's a mistake to rely on the liquidated-damages clause. A disgruntled seller can hire an attorney to challenge it, and you could spend a lot more money defending yourself in court.

Keep in mind that assigned purchase agreements tend to be rather iffy. There's a lot that can go wrong in the time between signing them and actually concluding a sale between the seller and the rebuyer. If the sale can't be concluded, the seller is, of course, likely to get angry. And you want some good cover when that happens.

Are There Any Big Problems with Assignments?

There's an inherent problem in using an assignment to flip a property. It's simply that when sellers discover that you're reselling the property at a substantial profit, most of them are likely to be unhappy. After all, they conclude, what are you adding to the deal? They feel that your profit should rightly go into their pocket.

Never mind the fact that for whatever reason, they couldn't get the price you're reselling for on their own. (If they could've, they would've.) What you're bringing to the transaction is your marketing expertise.

As a result, you could have an angry seller on your hands who may refuse to sign off on the deal unless he or she gets more money or, even worse, may want to take you to court. To help avoid just this sort of confrontation, it's important to inform the seller of what's going on.

TIP

Giving full disclosure to the seller (and the buyer) is the key to helping avoid some of the problems when using assignments.

Remember, even though what you do with property after you and the seller agree on a price shouldn't make any difference, it's better to let the seller know up front what's happening to avoid any problems later on.

Should I Disclose to the Buyer, Too?

I would. If you handle it wisely by letting the buyer know what you're paying for the property, there shouldn't be many problems. Indeed, the buyer may be impressed with your real estate acumen and want to work with you on a future deal!

On the other hand, if you conceal the information that you're tying up the property for a low price and reselling it at a higher one, and the buyer discovers this later on, he or she may think that you were trying to pull a fast one and go after you.

Keep in mind that most rebuyers won't care that you're flipping or how much you're making on the deal as long as they're assured that they aren't paying more than market price. If they see that they're getting a good deal, they will usually be satisfied.

Remember, the right way to handle a flip is to be sure that all parties know what you're doing (and get this in writing in case someone should later have an attack of memory failure).

Should I Do an Option or an Assignment?

I like options. I don't like assignments.

Options are more or less clean deals. Everything is on the table. Everyone tends to understand them.

Assignments offer more opportunity for hiding things. Fewer people really understand them. And the opportunities for problems to arise are greater.

Some investors successfully do both. As for me, I suggest that you look at options and stay away from assignments.

What if I Can't Cash Out?

Sometimes it's hard to find a rebuyer who has good enough credit to get a mortgage at almost 100 percent or who can come up with sufficient cash to make a big down payment for a smaller mortgage. Therefore, you may find that to make a deal, it's to your advantage to get a second mortgage on a flip.

This works in the same ways as described earlier for options and assignments. However, in this scenario, when it's time for you to get your money out of the deal, there isn't enough cash to make it happen. Therefore, you give the rebuyer a second mortgage. You then get paid so much a month until you get all your money back, which usually happens a few years down the road when the rebuyer sells the property or refinances it. (Alternatively, you could sell your second mortgage at a discount for cash. In the early years of the mortgage, however, you can expect the discount to be very heavy—as much as 50 percent—because the buyer of the mortgage assumes the risk that the rebuyer of the property won't keep making the payments.)

Of course, it goes without saying that you would want your rebuyer to be a good credit risk, because if he or she defaults on the loan, you won't get all of your money out of the second mortgage. Many investors "age" these second mortgages for six months to a year before selling them for cash. Aged mortgages have a much smaller discount.

What Should I Know about Price Manipulation?

The source of the increasingly common perception that flipping is a shady practice is that over the past few years, unscrupulous investors have, in the process of flipping properties, manipulated mortgages, appraisals, and, most importantly, prices. Rather than do the real work of the transaction—namely, finding properties that are selling below market—they purchased properties at their actual market price and then, through manipulation, sold them for above market price to unwary buyers. This was done, apparently, in cooperation with lenders, who secured higher appraisals than were warranted and made bigger loans than were justified. Often these properties were sold to poorer minority rebuyers who really didn't understand market values or know how high their payments would be. Subsequently, when these rebuyers couldn't make the stiff payments, they lost their houses to foreclosure.

That's where the real trouble started for these unscrupulous flippers. Almost all home mortgages are insured or guaranteed through the government or a government-related agency (FHA, VA, Fannie Mae, Freddie Mac, and so forth) in one way or another. When the government began taking these properties back, it found out what was happening and launched criminal investigations of the flippers.

This is not something you ever want to have happen to you. Always do the right thing. Start by finding undervalued properties—there are plenty of them out there to go around. Then let everyone know what's happening in the deal, and get legitimate loans and appraisals. You'll do the seller, the rebuyer, the government, and even yourself a big favor.

Should I Always Try to Flip a Property?

Sometimes you'll have a choice: either you can flip the property, or you can hold it. What should you do? The answer is that whenever you can flip a property, do it. Don't hang onto the property.

The reason is simple: for every flippable property you find, you'll find a dozen or more perfectly acceptable properties that you can hold. Finding holders is easy; finding flippers is hard.

Furthermore, you need the cash that flipping can generate. Holding properties tends to drain cash away. Often there is some small negative cash flow. And it can take years before you can get cash out of the holders in order to buy more properties.

There's really no big decision here. If you can generate cash from a flippable property, go for it. You can always find a holder tomorrow.

When Should I Check with My Attorney?

Flipping properties is a great way to make quick money in real estate. But it's loaded with pitfalls. Therefore, be sure to check with a good real estate attorney *before* trying any flip. This will cost you a few bucks, but it can also save you a lot of money and headaches in the long run.

Moving Up to Commercial Properties

For most real estate investors, commercial properties are a step up. Few start here; many more move up to this level.

In a way, getting started in commercial real estate is like starting all over again. There are new parameters to learn, and a new way to see real estate.

In this chapter we'll discuss the basics of getting started in investing in commercial property—what you need to know to get off the ground.

What Is Commercial Real Estate?

To many people, commercial real estate simply means retail space. They think of it as a shopping center or a strip mall—in other words, a place where commercial retailers (or sometimes wholesalers) are located.

However, in the trade, commercial real estate usually refers to much more than this. In essence, it's everything other than small residential rentals (houses, condos, and one- to four-unit apartment buildings). Here's a partial list of what might be considered commercial properties:

- Larger apartment buildings (over five units)
- Office buildings
- Self-storage facilities
- Agricultural land operations
- Land development
- Malls (large and small)
- Warehouse facilities
- Industrial sites
- Senior care facilities
- Motels and hotels
- Special-use facilities

TIP

Residential properties with four or fewer units qualify for owner-occupant financing; hence the distinction between four and under being residential and five and above being commercial.

While each of these different types of property has its own unique characteristics, there are some aspects of investing that most of them share. Three of these aspects are

1. Evaluation
2. Financing
3. Management

Evaluating Commercial Properties

There are a variety of methods for evaluating commercial property, including the cost of construction, comparative market analysis (CMA), price per square foot (for office buildings), price per front foot (for some retail space), and so on. However, the most commonly used method is that of income analysis or rate of return.

Income analysis uses the income that a property generates to come up with a figure for its value. Obviously, the greater the income, the more the property is worth.

TIP

With commercial property, the usual way to increase value is to increase the income the property generates while holding expenses in line. Increase the rental rate faster than expenses and this will be reflected in a more positive bottom line.

This makes sense, since commercial real estate is in competition with all other forms of investment. An investor can choose to invest in stocks, bonds, direct ownership of a company, and so on—or to invest in commercial real estate. The return that each type of investment generates, relative to the risk, usually determines where that investor's dollars will go.

Thus, when evaluating a piece of commercial property, what you want to do is to determine its rate of return. (Bare land held for development is an exception, since it normally generates little to no income while it is being held for development.)

The rate of return is called the "cap" rate and is usually calculated in this fashion. The gross income from a property (from rents and all other sources) is calculated on an annual basis. From this are subtracted all expenses, including maintenance, repair, vacancy, and so forth. (It's important to understand that debt servicing— interest, principal, depreciation, and so on—is *not* factored in here.)

This yields the net operating income (NOI). The NOI is then divided by the price of the property, and that yields the cap rate.

For example, if the net operating income of a property is $100,000 and the price is $1,000,000, the cap rate is 10 percent.

This can also be worked from another direction. If you know the cap rate expected for a particular type of investment and you know the NOI, you can come up with the price. For example, if the NOI is $50,000 and the expected cap rate is 10 percent, then the property's value should be $500,000.

TIP

Determining net operating income can be tricky. One method is to use an annual property operating data (APOD) sheet, which lists all expenses and income sources. An excellent version of an APOD sheet, as of this writing, is available for free from the Certified Commercial Investment Member Institute at www.ccim.com.

Difference between Residential and Commercial Evaluations

If you've come from a background of dealing in rental homes, this new method of evaluation may seem quite foreign. After all, for small residential real estate, the usual way of handling evaluations is the CMA. You determine the recent selling price of comparable homes, and from that you derive the market value of the subject property. Since most homes are used as habitat and don't produce income, the income approach is irrelevant.

However, since commercial property is used for business purposes (to generate income) and not habitat, the income approach is quite relevant here.

What's interesting is to compare the two approaches for a rental home. For example, you may have a home that shows a value of $500,000 using the CMA approach.

However, as a rental, the same property may have an NOI of only $20,000 (annualized). Assuming a cap rate of 9 percent, we come up with an evaluation of only $220,000.

Looking at it yet another way, if the property is valued at $500,000, that yields a cap rate of only 4 percent, something that few, if any, investors would welcome.

What this suggests is that from an income perspective, the property is grossly overvalued.

Why the disparity between the income valuation of a home and the CMA valuation? The answer, as suggested earlier, is that homes are valued not for the income they can produce, but for their commodity value as habitat. Between 2000 and 2006, a huge demand from both those who wanted to live in homes and those who were speculating in them drove prices up multiples of times— the "real estate bubble." As a result, homes came to be priced far above any realistic value based on income. Commodity demand as habitat overran income potential.

TRAP

Today it's still hard to find a home that can rent for a high enough amount to cover expenses. The net rental income is often a fraction of what it takes to support the property. This is because the property value is not based on cash flow. All of which is another reason not to buy a rental home to hold unless and until you can get a bargain on the price.

After the bubble burst, however, things returned more to earth. As prices fell, homes once again began to come more in line with their income-producing value. That meant that it was easier to buy them and rent them out for a profit.

Financing Commercial Properties

As with valuation, if you're used to small residential properties, financing commercial real estate will come as a shock. Instead of the 90 to 100 percent LTV (loan-to-value ratio) that has become common in the residential housing market, much lower LTVs are found in the commercial market. Indeed, the typical mortgage on a commercial property tends to have a 75 to 80 percent LTV. (The exception is bare land, where a 50 percent LTV may be more the rule.)

Let's be clear about what this means. If you buy a $400,000 home in which you intend to live, and you've got sterling credit, you can probably get a loan for between $360,000 and $400,000, depending on the credit market when you apply.

On the other hand, if you're buying a small commercial property for $400,000, you'll be more likely to get a mortgage for between $300,000 and $320,000. That's a big difference. (If you're looking for a commercial mortgage, try www.steelheadcapital.com or www.loopnet.com.)

This becomes especially important as the numbers get bigger. On a $4 million commercial property, you might need to come up with a million dollars or so as a down payment (75 percent LTV).

The truth of the matter is that with commercial property, the lenders want you to have much more "skin," or equity, in the deal—a much larger down payment. You'll find it increasingly hard to play the commercial mortgage game without putting in a fair amount of your own cash.

Of course, that's why there's secondary financing that helps with the down payment. It can take a variety of forms, from a simple second mortgage to equity involvement (as in a mezzanine loan). Today, mortgage brokers that specialize in second mortgages are plentiful. (Try www.hanovermc.com or www.steelhead capital.com.) Also, sellers will often carry back paper in order to facilitate a deal. With secondary financing, it is often possible to get a combined LTV (first and second mortgages) of 90 percent. In rare cases, that can go higher.

Demonstrating Cash Flow

In order to get financing on a commercial property, you really need two things. The first, which almost goes without saying, is a good credit report/credit score on yourself. If you have weak credit or a poor score, start thinking about a new line of investment.

The second thing you need is to be able to demonstrate viable cash flow from the property. Lenders know that in order for you to make the payments, your property must be able to generate sufficient funds to pay all expenses *plus* service the mortgage debt. They frequently use a formula called a debt service coverage ratio, or DSCR.

The DSCR is simply the ratio of net income (from cash flow) to debt on the property. Lenders are looking for a ratio of 1.15 to 1.25. In other words, when you divide *net* income (after all expenses, including vacancies) by the mortgage payment (debt servicing), the result should be 1.15 to 1.25. To put it another way, you need $1.15 to $1.25 of net income for each $1.00 of debt servicing. For a $100,000 annual mortgage payment, you need $115,000 to $125,000 of net income.

In order to get good financing, the property needs to be a cash cow. It needs to generate lots of income. You also need to get it at a good price, which translates into a lower mortgage (going back to cap rates noted earlier).

During the runup of most real estate prices between 2001 and 2006, it became increasingly difficult to find good financing for commercial properties—it simply wasn't possible to produce a satisfactory DSCR. However, since then, with the overall blowout of prices and the general decline in property values, once again it's possible in many cases to have sufficient cash flow from properties to secure good loans.

TRAP

It's a matter of perspective. Hard times for sellers of real estate can mean great bargain hunting for savvy buyers.

Managing Commercial Properties

Yet another requirement for success in commercial real state (not to mention success in getting financing) is the ability to handle management. Here a strong track record is desirable, whether in the type of commercial property you're acquiring or borrowed from another type of property. (All of which is why I always suggest getting started in small residential investments, where you can learn and acquire a beginning track record.)

Suppose you are interested in buying a mom-and-pop "board and care" assisted-living facility. Today these are one of the most popular means of moving into the commercial field. Essentially, you buy a home in a good neighborhood and convert it into an assisted-living facility, typically housing around six elderly residents.

Since these residents often pay a high rent for assisted living (anywhere from $1,500 to $7,000 monthly), the cash flow is enormous, meaning that the project has the potential to be highly profitable.

On the other hand, for this to be successful, it's necessary for you to be able to handle a wide variety of management tasks. You'll need to know something about health care, as you (or someone you hire or partner with) will be responsible for round-the-clock administration of medications and to some extent treatments such as physical therapy. This is in addition to the many different licensing requirements you need to comply with and the liability issues involved.

You'll also need to have knowledge of the hospitality industry (motels and hotels) because you'll be managing room cleaning, meals, laundry, and so forth.

And since you're using a conventional home, you'll need to be able to deal with local zoning boards to get either zoning changes or variances to allow the special use you want.

Thus management becomes a major issue. (You'll recall from Chapter 1 that Bob and Jane were committed to working at managing their small office building almost full-time in order to make it a success.) In addition to senior assisted-living facilities and office buildings, management is also critical for retail stores, self-storage facilities, shopping malls, warehouses, and motels and hotels.

Furthermore, it's not enough to be convinced in your own mind that you can handle the management burden. In order to get good financing to purchase a commercial property, you must demonstrate to a lender that you have a solution for its management needs. To repeat, when you are first starting out, that usually means showing that you personally are ready, capable, and willing to do the job yourself.

Location Is Critical

Of course, in residential real estate, we all learned that location cubed (location, location, location!) is the most important factor in determining value. It's also an important factor with commercial real estate.

For example, with retail space (shopping centers large and small), traffic flow (either in cars or by pedestrians) is critical. With hotels and motels, being on a major artery and close to an anchor (such as an airport) can make the difference between failure and survival. (Nothing is worse than a motel located on a side street!) With office buildings, being off the main drag, yet close to a source of customers can be just as important. For example, an office building that caters to medical practitioners should be near a hospital, one that attempts to rent space to legal professionals should be near a courthouse, and so on.

Special Needs

In addition, each type of commercial property has its own special requirements. For example, hotels and motels are typically rated by Michelin, AAA, Mobil, and other rating services. If you're going to be successful, you need a high rating (or else most potential customers will pass you by).

For retail space, you must be able to deal with your tenants' business cycles. Some commercial tenants do the majority of their business during the Christmas season. Others do most of it during the summer water-sport season. Still others do it during the winter ski season. During the on-season, these businesses are flush with cash and may be able to pay high rents. During the off-season, however, they may be struggling to survive. Your leases must reflect the reality of their business cycle—or else you'll drive them out.

TRAP

Beware of restaurants. If you buy property that you intend to rent to a restaurant or, riskiest of all endeavors, buy property in which to open your own restaurant, be aware that your chances of success are nearly nil. Most restaurants fail within their first year. Nearly 70 percent fail within their first three to five years. While for some strange reason it is most people's dream to open a "good restaurant," resist the impulse if you have it. Yes, a successful restaurant can be a gold mine. But an unsuccessful one definitely will be a money pit.

For land development, you'll need to determine whether you're going to build on the property yourself (often to suit tenants) or to hold the property until you can flip it (as when prices soar because of new surrounding development or other factors). That means handling either construction financing or long-term landholding financing.

In short, while there are many similarities among the different types of commercial real estate, every type has its own special

needs. To succeed, you'll need to be able to identify those needs—
and deal with them adequately.

I encourage you to get started in commercial real estate. To a large extent, it's where the really big money is. On the other hand, I suggest that you take it one step at a time. And the first step is to get going with small residential properties.

Alligators versus Cash Cows

This chapter grew out of an e-mail that I received at my Web site (www.RobertIrwin.com) from a reader complaining that he was having trouble getting a property's rental income to cover the mortgage and other expenses. "How do I know in advance whether a house I'm interested in buying is an alligator or a cash cow? And how do I reduce negative cash flow in a rental that I already own?" he asked.

Good questions.

An alligator is a property where the expenses are so high that you can't cover them with the rental income, so that your monthly losses (negative cash flow) eat you alive; hence the name. A cash cow is a property for which your rental income exceeds your expenses; each month, it gives you "milk" in the form of money in your pocket (positive cash flow).

In this chapter, we'll look at some solutions to the age-old problem of evaluating smaller residential property in terms of its cash flow. (For cash flow concerns with larger residential and commercial property, check the previous chapter.)

How Do I Calculate Income versus Expenses?

If you are planning to invest in a rental home, it's important that you understand exactly what your expenses are likely to be. If you already own investment property, you need to know at all times where you stand financially vis-à-vis your investment. (Income is much easier to estimate or determine—unless you have a vending machine or two, it's simply the total of your rents for the property.) A useful tool in both situations is the rental property income and expense sheet.

At the end of every month, for a rental property that you already own, you can draw up an income and expense report to help you gauge the status of your cash flow. These figures will give you a very exacting look at how well you did that month. If you haven't been sufficiently careful, your ledger could look like the one in Figure 1.

Figure 1 Monthly Rental Property Income and Expense Sheet

Income (from rent) $1,500		$1,500
Expenses		
Mortgage payment	$1,500	
Taxes	600	
Insurance	50	
Maintenance	50	
Repairs	50	
	2,250	−$2,250
Monthly cash loss		−750

This property is losing $750 cash a month before depreciation is calculated. That's a loss of $9,000 a year! Nobody in his or her right mind would want such an alligator. Indeed, this is the type of negative cash flow that eats you alive!

But, some readers may be wondering, what about tax shelters? Doesn't rental real estate provide some tax benefits for owners?

How Do I Calculate the Tax Benefit?

> Determining the tax benefits of owning a particular piece of real estate can be a task requiring a high level of expertise. The following discussion is intended strictly as an overview; it might not apply in your situation, is not advice, and should not be relied on. For tax advice and before making any move that would involve tax consequences, see a good accountant or tax attorney.
>
> NOTE

Like most people, you have probably heard that real estate investments can provide a tax shelter. Don't the tax advantages offset the monthly cash loss?

No, not entirely, at least not in most cases. It's true that you may get some tax advantages from owning rental property. Virtually all the expenses in our example (with the exception of the principal portion of the mortgage payment, that which repays the loan) can be used to offset your rental income for the purpose of determining your profit. When you add to that an amount for depreciation (a loss that occurs only on paper), your monthly expenses could exceed your monthly income, thus resulting in a loss. In some cases (see Chapter 13), that amount of loss might be deductible from your other taxed income.

It's important to understand that, when calculating your profit or loss, rental expenses must first be offset by rental income. You can't simply take all your rental property expenses as a deduction from your total taxable income from all sources combined. For your investment rental property, you first subtract your property expenses from your property income; if that reveals a loss, that loss may or may not be deductible from your total taxable income.

For the property in the example, we would have a $1,250 loss each month after depreciation. How much of a tax advantage is that?

Monthly Rental Property Income and Expenses, Including Depreciation

Monthly cash loss	−$750
Depreciation	−500
Total monthly expenses including depreciation	−$1,250

The tax advantage answer depends on several factors, including your total income and your marginal tax bracket. For now, let's just say that if your total annual income is $150,000 or higher, you will not be able to take any immediate tax deductions for your rental property. In other words, for practical purposes, there are no immediate tax-deduction advantages from investment property for those who are well off enough to make over $150,000 a year. (It all has to do with the "active-passive" rules of the tax code. Remember that this is a very superficial look at real estate taxation in which we are glossing over many of the details. Again, for a more detailed examination, check Chapter 13.)

If your annual income, on the other hand, is under $150,000, then you may be able to deduct at least a part of your loss from that year's income. In other words, the property will provide some tax benefit.

How big is the tax benefit likely to be? That's determined by your marginal tax bracket. The higher your bracket, the greater the benefit.

Let's say that you're in the 28 percent tax bracket. (Check with your accountant to see what your marginal bracket is—you might be surprised to find that it's lower than you think!) You could get 28 percent of the $1,250 monthly loss, or $350 a month, in our example. Doing so would yield the results shown in Figure 2.

Figure 2 Estimated Tax Savings

Monthly loss	$1,250
Tax bracket	× 28 percent
	350
Annualized	× 12 percent
	$4,200

On this property, assuming a 28 percent tax bracket, the actual tax savings for lower-income taxpayers (the amount you'll not have to pay in taxes) would be slightly over $4,000.

Being able to deduct $4,200 from your annual tax bill does help a lot to offset the $9,000 annual *cash* loss. Suddenly that loss is down to about $5,000. But even that is high, and most people would still consider a property with that much loss to be an alligator.

So the question becomes, how do you get that loss reduced so that you at least break even? In other words, how can a rental property owner deal with negative cash flow?

What about Increasing Rents?

If your rents aren't enough to cover expenses, why not just increase rents? The answer to that question depends on how much leeway there is between the rent that you are charging and the rent that most other rental property owners in your area are charging.

In the real world, in the open market for rental units, you are in competition with every other landlord-investor. Increase your rents beyond the prevailing market rates and you'll have nothing but vacancies.

That's the case once you already own the property. However, there are some things you can do to avoid a negative cash flow problem before you buy. For example, buy a less expensive property for which your mortgage, taxes, and insurance—that is, your expenses—will be lower than your rental income.

TIP

Your constant goal should be to buy a rental property at close to or better than break-even.

I'm sure many readers will be quick to point out that if you pay less for a property, you probably will get less rental income from it. So even though your expenses will go down (because of a lower purchase price), so will your rental income.

Yes and no. Renting is different from buying and selling. In the sale and purchase market, the price for each property is usually well defined, based on comparable sales.

With rentals it's less clear. For example, a three-bedroom, two-bath home may rent fairly consistently for around $1,000 in your area. However, homes with three bedrooms and two baths in that area, all of which may rent for that same $1,000, may sell for anywhere from $120,000 to $160,000. In other words, if you buy a three and two at the lower end of the price range, you'll very likely be able to rent it for roughly the same amount as you could if you had bought property at the upper end of the price range. Yet your monthly expenses will be far less in the lower-priced property. So one way to lower your monthly expenses is to "buy low" in the first place.

What about Cutting Expenses?

Assuming that you've done all you can to increase your rental income, is there anything else you can do to get closer to break-even on a property that you already own? Can you cut your expenses? That, of course, is the big question. Here are the answers using the property described earlier as an example.

Fixed Expenses

Taxes

There's very little you can do to cut your property taxes. It might be possible to have the property reassessed, but unless market values overall have dropped, a revaluation is just as likely to result in a higher assessment as in a lower one. This is most likely a fixed expense that you have to pay.

Insurance

Like taxes, insurance tends to be a fixed expense. You could shop around for a cheaper policy. But remember, in addition to fire insurance, as a landlord you also need high liability insurance in case a tenant gets hurt on the property and sues you. Again, there's probably little you can do here.

Maintenance

This item covers routine expenses such as paying the water bill and the lawn, pool, and garden care services. Actually, the $50 in our example is very low. It's unlikely that you'll be able to cut this figure significantly.

Repairs

This expense is actually a reserve. You put away 50 bucks a month so that when a $500 water heater goes out, you have the cash to pay for it. If the house is much older, $50 a month is probably not enough. You might have to put away several hundred dollars a month to be ready to repair a roof or a heating system. If the house is nearly new and in good shape, you might be able to reduce this reserve.

TIP

A wise investor will also keep a reserve for cleanup, rent-loss, and rent-up expenses. Most landlords assume that their house or condo, on average, will be vacant between two and four weeks a year as tenants come and go. Each time a tenant moves out, there's a cleanup expense. Then, until a new tenant moves in, there's a rent-loss expense. And finally, to find a new tenant, there's advertising, credit reports, and other rent-up expenses.

Variable Expense: The Mortgage

We are left with only one expense that we can control in some way: the mortgage payment.

We can reduce the mortgage payment in a variety of ways. We've already discussed buying a less expensive home and putting in more of your own cash.

Another way to reduce the mortgage payment is to get a lower interest rate. There are a variety of ways to do this. You can plan ahead so that if interest rates are high when you make your purchase, you go for an adjustable-rate loan. This type of loan typically begins with a "teaser" rate that is below market, often as much as 1 to 3 percent or more lower. The savings can be huge. Just keep in mind, however, that these teaser rates disappear rather quickly. Often within a year or two, your interest rate on the adjustable-rate loan will rise (reset) to market rate or even above. That's the time to refinance, if possible, to a lower-rate mortgage (or to resell).

On the other hand, if interest rates happen to be low when you buy, get a fixed-rate 30-year loan. This will lock in your mortgage at the low rate so that when interest rates rise, you won't find your monthly expenses going up.

With investment property, almost always go for either an interest-only mortgage or the longest-term amortized mortgage you can get—typically 30 years. The reason is your goal of low monthly payments to reduce your overall monthly expenses. Shorter-term amortized loans are sometimes written with a slightly lower interest rate and a greater return on equity, but the payments are always higher. Go for the long-term mortgage.

Can I Eliminate the PMI?

Yet another way to reduce the mortgage amount—and thereby reduce your monthly mortgage expense—is to get rid of the private mortgage insurance (PMI). In our examples, in which we obtained a low- to zero-down mortgage by being an owner-occupant, we glossed over the fact that these mortgages all require PMI. This insures the lender (not you, the borrower) against loss in case you fail to make your payments. You, however, pay the cost in the form of a higher interest rate, typically 3/8 to 3/4 percent more. This can add $100 or more to your monthly mortgage payment.

There are two ways to get rid of the PMI. The first is to prove to the lender that your home has appreciated in value to the point where the mortgage is less than 80 percent of the value. At that point, the lender should simply take off the PMI, which will lower your payments. However, it takes time for the value of your house to appreciate sufficiently, often many years. And lenders are notoriously slow in removing the PMI, even when removing it is obviously justified.

Another method is to refinance. Here you get two smaller loans instead of the original large one. You get a first mortgage for 80 percent of the value (remember, no PMI is required here) and a second mortgage for as much as possible, anywhere from 10 percent to the full remaining 20 percent of the property's current value. Hopefully the combined interest rate on the two mortgages will be less than the rate for the large single mortgage with PMI. Any good mortgage broker can run the numbers for you. (Also, check Chapter 10, where we'll go into financing in greater detail.)

Obviously, it's not going to be easy to cut the mortgage expense. But there is another way to do it: put more cash down.

Cutting the Monthly Payment by Putting More Money Down

It's important that you understand the relationship between how much you put into the property and your monthly expenses. The less of your own money you put into a property, the greater your leverage and, ultimately, your profits. However, your monthly expenses will be greater too, because you'll have a bigger mortgage.

On the other hand, the more of your own money you put into a property, the lower your mortgage payments will be—and the less difficulty you'll have in covering them with rental income. Put more down and you'll have lower mortgage payments, which, of course, are much easier to meet.

TRAP

Two of the biggest mistakes that first-time real estate investors make are to underestimate their mortgage expense and to overestimate their rental income.

But doesn't this fly in the face of the advice that says you should use other people's money (OPM)? The more of your own money you put in, the less of OPM you're using. Won't that reduce your profits?

Yes and no. Your profits will also be reduced if you need to put money into an alligator of a property each month to keep it out of foreclosure (in other words, if you need to make huge payments that are not covered by rental income). Put less money down, and you might get nickeled-and-dimed to death.

It's important to remember that buying and renting real estate is a balancing act. The closer you get to break-even, the better an investment your property is. The ideal rental investment, in fact, will break even or produce a positive cash flow.

Thus, use as much of OPM as you can. But balance that with your own money (after buying right and getting the lowest mortgage payment possible through wise financing).

Is There Any Other Time when Putting in More Cash Makes Sense?

As we've said, if you can find a property that offers high rent with low expenses and you finance the property wisely, you can get by with putting in little or no cash of your own. On the other hand, if you buy a property with a lower rental income and higher payments, you'll want to put your money into it to reduce the mortgage amount to a level where the monthly payments are balanced by the rental income.

Sometimes, however, your goal is not simply to rent the property out, but to turn it over for a big profit. When properties are appreciating rapidly, you may need a time frame of only a year or two, sometimes much less. During that time, you hope to resell for a big profit, to make a killing on a market upswing. So you may overlook the goal of buying close to break-even and instead buy a property for which the rental income doesn't come close to meeting the expenses. In this sort of situation, putting in a lot of cash to keep the mortgage payments low can make sense.

Think of it this way: if you have the cash, what else would you do with it? Your choices are limited, typically, to stocks, bonds, and interest-bearing deposits. Chances are that you'll make far more on it by putting it into a piece of real estate that has the potential to generate a quick profit. (Besides, with lots of cash and a quick buy, you can sometimes persuade the seller to reduce the price significantly.)

I've known investors who would put as much as 50 percent, or sometimes even 100 percent, down with the intent of reselling within a short time frame. Ultimately, your decisions will line up with your investment goals and market conditions.

As we've seen, you can determine a property's cash flow by careful analysis before you buy. If you need to lower a negative cash flow for a property you already own, you can do so in the ways suggested. However, always keep in mind that some properties simply will never break even or produce a positive cash flow no matter what you do, short of paying the entire price for them in cash. Those are alligators to avoid.

Finding Good Starter Properties

There are more than 65 million homes in the United States, and the vast majority of them are single-family dwellings. For the beginning investor, this inventory represents a huge treasure trove of getting-started properties. They are everywhere. To find the best one for you, you just have to know how to sift through the pile.

Before jumping in, however, it's important to clearly define what we're looking for. As we saw in the first chapter, a house makes a great first investment, probably the best there is. However, it's not just any house that we want—it's a house that we can make a profit on. That means that we must be able to buy it inexpensively. The ideal investment property will sell for below market price. Where do we find it?

In this chapter we're going to consider two areas:

1. Properties listed with local agents
2. Properties listed as "for sale by owner" (FSBOs)

Hidden Treasures in the Listings

In any endeavor, it's important to take advantage of what's already out there to help you. In other words, if you want to build a wheelbarrow, it's wise not to set about reinventing the wheel.

Already in place is a vast network of listed properties. Indeed, at any given time, probably around 85 percent of the properties that are for sale are listed with agents. So the first step is to tap into this resource.

TIP

As a buyer, unless you're using a buyer's broker (discussed in Chapter 11), you probably won't have to pay a commission on your purchase—that's the seller's problem. So, if you find a good one, why not buy a listed property?

I've heard many beginning investors say something like, "There's nothing good listed. If there were, an agent would already have bought it!" That's a mistake in thinking. Normally there are so many properties for sale at any given time that there are bargains out there just waiting to be discovered. Furthermore, every agent I've ever known would much rather get a commission, which means immediate income, than buy a listed property, which means a long-term investment. Agents need that constant influx of cash that commissions supply if they are to survive. Normally, they buy for investment only as a last resort.

All of which is to say that a person who complains about the lack of bargains in listings probably hasn't taken the time to look.

Only after you've spent a month or two checking out all currently listed properties in your area should you conclude that there's nothing for you in the MLS.

Work with an Agent

As noted earlier, since it's not likely to cost you anything, you'll want to work with an agent, one who has access to the Multiple Listing Service (MLS) in your area. Agents who have MLS access are Realtor members of the National Association of Realtors. (You can also find listed properties on your own by using the Internet and going to www.realtor.com, where virtually all properties found on the MLS are listed.)

Tell your agent exactly what you're interested in. If you're just getting started, like Bob and Jane in the first chapter, chances are that you're looking for a house both as a place to live and as an investment. You have your choice of the greatest selection of properties on the MLS.

Also, keep in mind the criteria for an investment/rental property that we discussed in detail in Chapter 1; now look for bargains, or those where the sellers have indicated that they are willing to negotiate.

Criteria for Good Resale/Rental Investment Properties (from Chapter 1)

1. Look for good neighborhood schools.
2. Check for pride of ownership in the neighborhood.
3. Aim for a low crime rate in the neighborhood.
4. Be sure to buy close to shopping and with access to transportation.
5. Buy not too big and not too small.
6. Look for an active rental market in the area.

7. Make sure it's a house that is suitable for tenants.
8. Get a house that is easily maintained without lots of repairs.
9. Buy close to home (the extra criterion).

Look for Stale Listings

Stale properties are those that have been listed the longest. A seller who puts a property on the market on Monday isn't likely to cut his or her price by Friday. On the other hand, a seller who's had his or her property on the market for three months with no activity is likely to be very anxious to make a deal—and be willing to cut his or her price to do it.

TIP

A typical listing contract is written for 90 days. Toward the end of that time, the agent is likely to put pressure on the seller to accept any offer. After all, if the seller decides not to renew the contract after 90 days, the agent will lose the listing—and a commission.

In a normal market, a large number of properties will be in the stale category. Indeed, most properties will take three to six months or more to sell. In a slow market, you'll want to extend your time frame to homes that have gone unsold for six months or longer. In a hot market, however, you will have to reduce that time frame.

Look for Price Reductions

Another indication that a seller is anxious to dump a property is a price reduction, particularly a large reduction. A seller who cuts the price by $1,000 is merely trying to attract attention. A seller who cuts the price by $10,000 is serious.

Multiple price reductions—particularly when they come in close succession—indicate a very anxious seller. I once bought a home from sellers who were so anxious to sell that they were cutting their price by $10,000 a week until they finally sold the property. If I had waited long enough, I might have gotten the property for nothing! On the other hand, someone else certainly would have bought it long before then.

When you find a property that has been reduced in price and that otherwise seems suitable (see the criteria discussed previously), don't feel that you have to offer the current asking price. Just because a seller has reduced the price doesn't mean the price is at rock bottom. Treat a reduced price as you would any other—the starting point for negotiations. Work down from there.

Check for Clues in the Listings

Listing agents have a duty to protect their clients (in this case, the sellers), and they should do everything they can to attract buyers. This means letting buyers know when sellers are highly motivated to sell, which they often accomplish by writing clues into the listing.

Look for phrases such as "highly motivated" or "bring in all offers" or "wants to move immediately." You get the idea: the agent is sending out the word that this seller is very anxious and will consider lowball offers. If the property is also listed with price reductions, you probably have a real opportunity in the making.

Check Out the Properties

While this may seem simple-minded, the fact is that some beginning investors prefer the paperwork to the legwork. They will find a property that looks terrific on paper and make an offer.

Another mistake: real estate properties are not homogeneous. That means that every property has unique characteristics. No matter how good a property looks on paper or on the Internet, you have to check it out physically before you make an offer for it. You might find that this terrific property backs up to a dump site. Or that it has high-tension electric wires traveling over the fence line. Or that the street in front is all broken up and the city has no plans to fix it. Or . . . Nothing takes the place of looking at a property.

Look for FSBOs

Not all properties are listed. Some are being sold by their owners direct to sellers as FSBOs. When they see such listings, many beginning investors immediately jump to the conclusion that because there is no agent's commission involved, these listings must be bargains. Beware: in most cases, they are far from bargains. What you're looking for is the occasional FSBO that can make you a profit.

TIP

Most FSBO sellers plan on pocketing the money they expect to save by not going through an agent. The last thing in their minds is selling the property to you, the investment buyer, for less. Therefore, you need to find that FSBO seller who has common sense and will give you the money saved in order to get a quick sale.

Drive through Neighborhoods to Find FSBO Starters

The old tried-and-true method of finding FSBOs is to search your local neighborhoods. Drive through looking for "By Owner" signs. The modern method is to search the Internet, where most FSBOs are now listed. Check out these Web sites:

www.owners.com
www.fsbo.com
www.forsalebyowner.com

Think of yours and nearby neighborhoods as your "farm." You'll drive or check the Internet sites for homes for sale by owner in them on a fairly regular basis. When you find an FSBO that looks suitable, based on the criteria at the beginning of this chapter, stop by the property and engage the seller-owner in discussion. Find out what the asking price is and if there are any special features. Then check it out—do a comparative market analysis (CMA). Chances are you'll find that the FSBO price is at, or maybe even a little higher than, market price!

"How can a seller even think that?" you may be asking yourself. "Why would I want to spend as much on a property without the benefit of an agent as I would with an agent?"

The reason the price is so high is that, quite frankly, most FSBO sellers don't think about the work involved in selling their property as much as they do about saving a big commission. Hence, they price their homes unrealistically.

Look for the Realistic FSBO Seller

You will occasionally find an FSBO seller who sees the light. He or she has priced his or her home below market in order to attract buyers. Rather than attempting to save a commission, this seller will give the commission, or at least part of it, to the buyer in the form of a lower price. The motivation: to get a quicker sale. This is someone with whom you can reason—and negotiate.

This is not to say that you should immediately pay the full asking price, even if it is below market. You should still negotiate, even lowball. But it's much better to start with a realistic seller than with a seller who thinks his or her property is so wonderful that you ought to pay full price, or more, for it.

Keep in mind, however, that buying a FSBO can be a challenge. You don't have an agent to handle the paperwork and other details. Many investment buyers in this situation will find it advisable to hire a fee-for-service attorney or agent to handle the paperwork for them. This probably will cost only around $1,000, and, if you're new to real estate investing, it can be well worth the money.

Carefully Check Out the Internet

In truth, this is probably the place you should start when you're looking for a good starter investment property. As noted, today virtually every property that's listed with an agent or that is being sold FSBO is also listed somewhere on the Internet. FSBO sites offer numerous tips and hints for working the FSBO market.

Advantages of Working the Internet

1. Easily viewed listings of almost all houses that are available
2. Color pictures of the homes listed, sometimes with virtual tours as well
3. Textual descriptions, including lot and house sizes, and number of bedrooms and baths
4. Location of the property, often including a map showing how to get there
5. E-mail addresses and phone numbers so that you can communicate with the sellers directly
6. Tips, hints, and other educational information
7. Financing, agent, attorney, and other links
8. And much, much more

The Internet can also help you find external information. There are dozens of Web sites that will help you locate comparables sold in the neighborhood (check www.zillow.com for free information). Many real estate sites offer information on schools and crime, title reports, and home inspectors. It's simply a matter of locating a Web site that caters to what you need.

It should be obvious from this that you can scan dozens, if not hundreds, of listings very quickly from the comfort of your computer room. This tends to be far more efficient than trying to look at a listing book in an agent's office. It's certainly more efficient than touring streets hunting for FSBO signs.

On the other hand, once you find a listing you are interested in, it again becomes a physical game. It's very important that you take the time to visit the property at least once. On the Internet, you cannot actually see the property or the neighborhood. To tell if it's really a good buy, you must do the same sort of fieldwork that you would do for a paper MLS listing. You have to go to the property and check it out. Talk to the owner or agent. You'll quickly discover what the real truth about the property is.

Before you buy, you must view the property directly, physically. This is critically important.

The Bottom Line

Whether MLS listings or FSBOs, the properties offered for sale are the happy hunting ground of real estate investors. Whether you search the physical world or the cyber world, you should be able to find just the starter property you want.

Maximizing Rental Potential

At some point, every investor in real estate becomes a landlord. It's inevitable that if you hold a property, you'll need to rent it out to obtain income from it—income to pay your mortgage, taxes, insurance, repairs, maintenance, and so on.

As a landlord, it will be up to you to find tenants, collect rents, clean up when tenants move out, and maintain and repair your properties. How well you do this will determine, to a large extent, how well you succeed in real estate.

In this chapter, we'll go into the basics of what you need to know to be successful at residential rentals. (See Chapter 6 for more information on commercial rentals.)

We'll see what makes a good rental and how to keep it profitable:

- How to find a good rental property
- How to find good tenants
- How to keep good tenants
- How to profit from rentals

How Do I Find a Good Rental Property?

As noted in the first chapter, there are certain criteria that you can look for to help you determine whether a home will make a good rental. If the property has these criteria, then chances are that it will. If it doesn't, you'd be better off looking elsewhere.

Basic Rental Property Criteria

- Good schools
- A low crime rate in the neighborhood
- Close to shopping and with access to transportation
- Not too big and not too small
- An active rental market in the area
- A house that is suitable for tenants
- A house that is easily maintained without lots of repairs

In addition, there are certain other elements that, if you find them, can only be a plus.

The Area Has an Appropriate Tenant Base

You should look in areas where the type of property is suitable for the local workforce. For example, if you have a low-income property and most of the local workforce consists of highly paid white-collar workers, you might not find tenants easily. Similarly, if you have blue-collar workers in the area, you might have trouble finding tenants for a high-priced property. The property should match the tenant base.

There's a Real Shortage of Rentals

Ideally, yours will be the only rental in the area. Obviously, that's not going to happen. But if there are too many rentals chasing too few tenants, you'll have trouble. Check local newspapers for "For Rent" ads to get a sense of the supply. Also, visit a few of these rentals to learn what your competition is. And ask a few real estate agents who specialize in rental properties what the rental market is like.

Homes in the Area Offer a Good Ratio of Rental Income to Cost

Look for properties that offer a good ratio of rental income to cost. This is tricky. You want your monthly income from rents to at least come close to covering your expenses (reread Chapter 7 if you're not sure why). The only way you can do this is to avoid overpaying for the property, which means that you'll want relatively "cheap" rentals.

The Rental Is Close to Your Home

There's one last, but vitally important, criterion that we also discussed in the first chapter: buy close to your own home.

TRAP

The single biggest mistake an investor can make is to buy rental property at a distance. It turns renting up, collecting rents, and handling maintenance and repairs into a nightmare.

I made the mistake of buying at a distance when I first started in real estate, and I paid a price for it. Chances are, as you read this, you'll be nodding to yourself and saying, okay, that's his opinion. Let's move on.

The problem here is that until they've experienced it, most people simply don't believe this is as serious a concern as it is. Then they can't believe how much trouble they're in.

If there's only one thing about rentals that you get from this book, it should be, don't buy rental properties far from home (no more than half an hour away). That's how important I think this advice is.

How Do I Find Good Tenants?

Some investors complain that it's harder to find a good tenant than to find a good rental property! I don't believe that's the case. I've rented properties for more than three decades, and with only a few exceptions, I've always had good tenants. The simple rule here is that if you check out your tenants before you rent to them, you will avoid problems later on.

TIP

There are strict antidiscrimination laws covering renting. Get a complete set from HUD (800-767-7468) or from an agent or local rental service. Some of the rules state that you can't discriminate in renting because of race, religion, sexual preference, occupation, educational status, medical status, or age of the tenant(s). You also can't refuse to rent to tenants with children if the home is big enough. You can, however, refuse to rent because of the financial condition of the tenants, provided that you apply your financial criteria across the board equally to everyone who applies.

How do you check out prospective tenants? You talk to them and get them to fill out a thorough rental application. (These are available from various Web sites. Try www.Thelpa.com. But no matter where you get the forms, have your attorney check them out for appropriateness to your situation and area.) The application usually includes permissions for you to run a credit check, contact current employers, and call previous landlords. When people apply to rent a house or apartment from you, there are five main things to look for.

1. Adequate Credit

Don't expect that all of your tenants will have sterling credit. Indeed, if they were wonderful credit risks, they probably would be owners, not tenants. Instead, look for a history of making payments on time. If the applicant doesn't make timely payments on other bills, chances are that the rent will be late too. You can get a credit report (or be directed to how to get one) from one of the many landlord online services such as www.thelpa.com or www.mrlandlord.com. You can also have a local real estate agent run one for you. (Remember, you must have the applicant's permission to do this.)

2. Previous Landlords' Recommendation

Make this call, and make sure you don't just make it to the current landlord (who may be willing to tell you anything to get rid of a bad tenant!). Most landlords will be unwilling to go into detail, but one question that almost all will answer is, "Would you rent to this person again?" The answer can be very telling. (Remember, you should have permission to make this call.)

3. A Good Fit

If you have a big house, expect to rent to families with kids. If yours is a small place, be sure you don't get too many bodies in it. Also, keep track of the number of cars and motorcycles that tenants have. Too many will clog driveways and can become an eyesore. (There are federal and possibly state and local rules regulating how many bodies you can fit into a house—usually far more than you want!)

4. A Gut Feeling That Says Yes!

Trust your instincts. When you talk with prospective tenants, how do you feel about them? Do they seem like people who are likely to make the rent payments on time and keep the place up? Or do they seem like vagabonds who are interested only in getting in quickly and then paying slowly (or not at all) and messing up your place? I've found that heeding my gut feelings is often the best way to predict tenant behavior.

5. Sufficient Income to Make the Payments

A tenant who doesn't have a job probably can't make the rent payments no matter how good his or her credit report seems. You'll want to call the current employer and verify the length of employment, likelihood of continued employment, and salary. (Be sure your application, signed by the prospective tenant, gives you permission to make this call.) Employers won't normally tell you an employee's salary, but they will usually confirm a number that you give to them.

Offer a Clean Rental

In addition to the techniques just mentioned, you'll also want to be sure that you offer a good, clean rental. This means that the walls have been freshly painted (or at least cleaned), the carpet is without stains and dirt, the appliances have been cleaned, and so forth. (It costs only about a hundred dollars to have a professional cleaning crew make a place spotless in just a few hours.)

The theory here is that if you have a dirty apartment, you won't find a clean tenant who will want to rent it. Rather, the only people who will rent a dirty apartment are tenants who won't keep things clean. The way to find a clean tenant is to start out with a clean rental. It will appeal to the right kind of tenant for you.

How Much Should I Charge?

As noted in the first chapter, it's a good idea to charge a little below the prevailing market rates. For example, if rentals similar to yours are going for $2,000 a month, rent yours out for $1,900 or $1,950.

Obviously, you're going to rent faster because of the cheaper rent. But you'll also appeal to those tenants who are savvy about the market and know a good thing when they see it. In other words, a rental at slightly less than market often attracts a better tenant.

You can find out what similar properties are going for by becoming a pretend tenant for a weekend. Check out the rental properties in your area by going to see them. Talk to the owners. You can identify yourself as a landlord. Most other landlords will be happy to chat.

TIP

Check to see if there's a landlords' association in your area. Many areas have them. Consider joining or at least talking to some of the members to share information. This group can be particularly helpful in alerting you to bad tenants who may be in the area (those who move in, don't pay, mess up the property, and need to be evicted). Also check out the Internet. Consider joining www.landlordassociation.org or www.thelpa.com.

Should I Ask for the Money Up Front?

First-time landlords are sometimes hesitant about asking directly for their rent. Don't be. You're in the business of collecting rents, and you can't be shy about it. This is particularly the case when you're selecting a new tenant.

I always ask for a substantial deposit. The deposit should go toward both the cleaning of the property after the tenant leaves and maintaining the security of the rental (in case there's damage or failure to pay rent).

There's much confusion about deposits. Technically, in most states, the money you receive from a cleaning deposit is yours to spend when you receive it. However, when the tenant moves out, you're under an obligation to pay it back, provided that the tenant leaves the premises reasonably clean and without damage.

TIP
Some states require a landlord to keep deposits in a separate trust account and even to pay the tenants interest on the money. Check with a good agent who handles rentals in your area to find out if this applies to you.

The trouble that many landlords get themselves into is that they spend the deposits as soon as they get them. Then they don't have the money on hand to pay back the tenants when they move out. Landlords in this situation often try to rerent quickly and get a new deposit from a new tenant in order to repay the old. This is a kind of trap that it's best to avoid. Even if the state doesn't require it, I always keep tenants' deposits in a separate account, ready to return to them when required.

TIP
Most states require landlords to give a full accounting of deposits and pay back any unused portion within two to three weeks after the tenant moves out.

How Big Should the Tenants' Deposit Be?

The answer is, as big as possible. The more money the tenants put up as a deposit, the more responsible they are likely to be. They will always be eyeing that big deposit at the end of the tenancy, anticipating getting it back.

Many states, however, limit the maximum deposit amount, sometimes to one and a half or two times the monthly rental. In addition, there's also a limit on how much you can reasonably expect a tenant to come up with. For example, if your rent is $1,500 a month and you demand a $3,000 cleaning deposit, that's $4,500 to move in. You simply may not find that many tenants who have that much cash available. Thus, you may find that you're charging a smaller cleaning deposit in order to attract tenants.

Again, always ask for the deposit up front. Never allow the tenants to move in without paying all of it. A tenant who moves in having paid no deposit (or having made only a partial payment) will feel less pressure to look out for your premises. The deposit is your leverage, and you don't want to lose it.

Also, always get the first month's rent (or first and last if you're using a conventional lease) up front. Don't let the tenant move in with a partial payment.

The reason for getting the money up front may not seem obvious until you've been a landlord for a while and a future tenant pleads with you to accept partial payment. He or she may owe $2,500 to move in, but has only $1,250. Landlord, won't you please accept the $1,250 with the rest promised in only a week or two?

No, don't do it. A tenant who can't pay all the "move-in" money up front probably won't be able to make the monthly payments as they come due. This is an important rule not to overlook.

How Do I Keep Good Tenants?

You keep good tenants, once you have them, by making them happy. That may sound difficult, but it really isn't. Here are some easy-to-use guidelines that really do work.

Stay Out of Their Hair

Yes, come by once a month to collect the rent (unless they mail it in advance) and check out the property. But don't be there more often. They've rented the place, and they are entitled to "quiet enjoyment" of it. No tenant likes a snoopy landlord, and many will move out if you're too nosy. Leave your tenants alone, for the most part, and you'll do well. Of course, this applies only to those tenants who pay well and keep the place clean. It's a different story for bad tenants.

Always Take the Tenants' Calls

Usually tenants don't want to be your bosom buddy, so they will call only when there's a problem. But when there is a problem, they want someone to be on the other end of the line. You can maintain an answering service, an answering machine, or a cell phone.

But be sure that when the tenant calls, you either answer the phone or get back to him or her in a very timely fashion.

Fix Problems Fast

When the tenant calls, the problem could be a leaky faucet, a broken window, a stove that doesn't work, a dishwasher that spills water on the floor, or anything else. What you must do is quickly determine if the problem is the property's fault or the tenant's fault. And usually you can't do this unless you zip out there to take a look. (Remember, you bought close to home, right?)

Once you're there, if it's the tenant's fault, explain that you'll have it fixed right away, but the tenant will have to pay for it. The money will come from the deposit, but then the tenant will have to pay to bring the deposit back up to its full level.

If it's the property's fault (such as a broken hot water heater), tell the tenant that you'll fix it at your cost. And fix it immediately, within hours. While you might be willing to stay in a house without hot water (or whatever the problem is), tenants who are paying rent won't be. They expect things to be fixed as soon as humanly possible. And unless you want to lose them, you'll see that it's, in fact, done just that fast.

Make Regular Upgrades to the House's Fixtures and Features

Things do wear out. Carpets get holes in them. Paint fades and gets dirty. None of these things are the fault of the tenant. They're just wear and tear caused by normal living. And you should plan on upgrading your rental over time. Some landlords do this every five years, others every three, and still others every seven. The whole idea is that if the tenant moves out because the place is run down as a result of your lack of maintenance, it's going to cost you more money (in advertising, lost rents, your time, and so on) than it would have if you had fixed it to begin with. And you'll need to spruce up the place for a new tenant anyway. Therefore, spend the money and keep the existing good tenant.

Avoid Being an Arrogant Landlord

What many unsuccessful landlords do is become arrogant. They feel that because they are the property owner, the lowly tenant should bow before them. Sort of like saying that the tenant should be grateful to the landlord for providing a roof over his or her head.

That kind of thinking may have prevailed during the Middle Ages, but it has no place in modern-day life. Rather, the landlord-tenant relationship is one of mutual benefit. You provide the housing; the tenant provides the rents. Neither is superior in some strange way to the other. If you don't like the tenant, you can ask him or her to move. You can also raise the rent.

If the tenants don't like you or the rents you charge, they can move elsewhere. In short, tenants and landlords need each other.

If you can remember that this is strictly a business arrangement, you'll do better as a landlord.

How Do I Increase Profits from Rentals?

As we've seen, profits from real estate usually come from selling it for more than you paid. Inflation and shortages in the supply of housing (and other types of real estate) force prices up, and that allows you to make your profit.

However, there's another way to make money in real estate that we've only touched upon, and that's by collecting rents. When your rents are higher than your total expenses, you have positive cash flow. As that increases and you put more and more money in your pocket, you begin to make money from your rentals.

Generally speaking, when you buy a property, you lock in your expenses. (An exception would be if you have an adjustable-rate mortgage, where the interest rate and the monthly payment can fluctuate.) You do not, however, lock in your rental income. Over time, it should go up at least as fast as inflation, and, if there's a shortage of rental property in the area, it should go up faster as a result of demand pressure. The way you take advantage of this is to raise rents.

When Do I Raise Rents?

You raise rents when you can justify it given the rental market. Note that I didn't say that you raise rents when you need more money, or when your have unexpected repairs, or when you think the tenant deserves to pay more. All these are irrelevant to your rental rate. The amount of rent you can charge depends entirely on what other landlords in your area are charging for rents. When rates go up overall, you can raise yours, too.

TIP Rental rates usually go up when a tenant moves out and the landlord rents the unit to the next tenant for more. This has a ripple effect across the market.

However, you can sometimes raise your rents for an existing tenant to slightly above the market rate.

Remember that we said that it makes sense to rent for slightly below the market rate in order to rent the property to a good tenant quickly. Once that tenant has been in your unit for a year or so, however, some degree of inertia begins to take effect. It becomes an effort for the tenant to move out. There's the hassle of finding a new house or apartment; of dealing with the movers; of changing the utilities, mail, and phone; and on and on. In other words, all things being equal, tenants who are basically happy with where they live would rather not move if they could choose not to do so.

Of course, if you raise their rent, they'll reconsider. They'll immediately go out and see what else is available. They'll comparison-shop.

If other similar units are renting for more, they most likely will stay with you. If other similar units are renting for about the same amount, they probably will stay with you.

However, if other similar units are renting for just a little bit less, the chances are that they will still stay with you simply to avoid the hassle of moving.

Thus, if you raise the rent from $950 to $1,000 when similar units are renting for $975, most tenants will pay the extra amount. It's simply easier than moving.

TIP

Avoid big rent increases because they unnerve tenants and make them more likely to jump ship. Also, try to do something for the tenant, such as repainting or recarpeting, before you raise the rent.

As you can see, if you're very careful, once you have the tenant settled in, you can sometimes raise the rent and charge an above-market rental rate. Push it too far, however, and you'll lose the tenant.

How Do I Get Rid of Bad Tenants?

Bad tenants usually fall into two categories: either they pay late (or don't pay at all), or they make a mess of the property. Chronic behavior of one or both types suggests that you may be better off without the tenant. (Sometimes you simply want to get rid of a tenant to put yourself in a better state of mental health!)

If you have a month-to-month tenancy, a 30-day notice to move is normally all it takes. (Some states require a longer notification period in certain cases, such as if the tenant has rented for a year or longer.) With a lease, however, the tenant has the right to keep the property (as long as the conditions of the lease are met) until the term is up, often a year or more. To get rid of a bad tenant with a lease, you may actually have to pay him or her off. This could mean giving the tenant several months' rent to move out. (You'd do this only for a tenant you really couldn't stand.)

Of course, the ultimate way to remove a tenant who won't pay is eviction. This involves an unlawful-detainer court action. You'll need an attorney at least the first time you try it.

If you "mind the store" and raise rents when appropriate, keep good tenants, and get rid of bad ones, over time you'll find that your rewards in the form of positive cash flow from your rental property will positively amaze you.

Residential Financing for Small Investors

The eternal question for investors is, "How do I get a good mortgage when I buy?"

When dealing with small residential properties (houses, condos, and one- to four-unit apartment buildings), the answer continues to be, "Move in."

For owner-occupants with a good credit history and adequate income, loans are available with a loan-to-value (LTV) ratio as high as 100 percent or more (for "conforming" loans, as of this writing). If you are prepared to live in the property, the very best financing in the world is available to you.

Of course, if you want to later convert the property to a rental, you may wonder how long you must live in the property to justify being an owner-occupant.

Unfortunately, I've never found a hard-and-fast answer. Some mortgage experts say it all comes down to intent: you must intend to move in. Whether you actually do so is another matter.

Others say that living in the property for six months to a year is sufficient. Still others say two years.

Nevertheless, if you go to a mortgage broker, bank, or other institutional lender and let it know that you want to buy a house to occupy, the doors to the money vault will swing open. There's nothing else like it in the world of real estate financing.

Owner-Occupant Means Occupying the Property

It's important to understand, however, that we're not talking here about *pretending* to be an owner-occupant. We're talking about actually moving into the home and living there—occupying it.

The great temptation for investors is to say that they will live in the property in order to get the good financing and then not actually move in. By so doing, they take advantage of better financing than they could get as an investor. The reason for not moving in, of course, is that they may already have a house in which they live and they don't want to lose even a month's worth of rent from the property they are buying.

No matter what you call this, it's simply a no-no. If you don't move in, it could land you in hot water. Lenders are on the alert for people who say they are moving in when in reality they intend to rent out the property. To confirm that you've moved in, a lender may call after a month or two to check. Or it may send your payment books to your attention at the new home's address with "no forwarding" requested. Or it may even send someone by three months later to see how you're doing. If a tenant answers the door, the ruse is up.

Almost all mortgages are in some way insured, guaranteed, or resold through government or quasi-government agencies. That means that if you lie and are caught, you will have to do a lot of explaining to the Treasury Department. Penalties could be anything from a demand that you repay the full amount of the loan immediately to an indictment on criminal charges.

All of which is to say that if you're going to put down that you intend to occupy the property in order to get a really great mortgage, be sure you in fact do that. Later on, after you've lived there for a while, you can think about converting it to a rental.

Are Nonoccupant Investor Mortgages Available?

They certainly are. Although the LTV, the borrower's qualifications, and the interest rates change from time to time, generally speaking these loans require a bigger down payment and a higher personal income, and they are sometimes written at a slightly higher rate of interest and more points.

Traditionally, residential investor mortgages require 20 percent down (an 80 percent LTV). Over the last few years, however, investor mortgages on one- to four-unit residential properties have become available with only 10 percent down (an LTV ratio of 90 percent). After the mortgage industry meltdown in 2007, however, it remains unclear whether these will still be available. Check with a good mortgage broker.

Higher Qualifying Income

Additionally, there's a little trick that lenders use for residential investors. They may not allow you to apply all of the income from the subject property toward qualifying for the mortgage.

In other words, they will count only about 75 to 85 percent of the income, yet at the same time they will count all of the expenses. As a result, the cash flow for the property will be reduced (for qualifying purposes). All of which means that you'll need more personal income to qualify for the purchase.

That means that even if your property breaks even, you still need some extra income of your own in order to balance out the expenses. This becomes even more of a problem the more properties you acquire. Each time you buy, since not all of the property's income is counted toward qualifying, you need ever-higher personal income levels. This is just another hurdle to overcome.

Where Do I Get Investor Financing?

You obtain an investor mortgage from the same place you get an owner-occupant loan—a mortgage broker, bank, or other lender. You simply state what you want the loan for, and the lender should do all the paperwork.

In addition, there's also the option of financing the property through the seller, which we'll discuss shortly.

How Do I Get Cash Out?

In the past, this was the single most difficult problem for the small investor. You might have owned a solid rental property that was producing a positive cash flow. Yet when you wanted to cash out some of your equity, lenders would simply turn their backs on you.

Today, it's a somewhat different story. In many cases, you can get an 80 percent mortgage including cash back to you. In some cases, 90 percent is available with cash back on a refinancing. But you do have to search around. Of course, you'll pay a stiffer interest rate and more points, and you will need more personal income to qualify. But at least the ability to refinance is there.

An alternative to the preceding scenario involves obtaining an institutional second mortgage. Many lenders offer these loans to investors. Generally speaking, the combined loan-to-value (CLTV) ratio is the same as it would be for a large first mortgage—80 to 90 percent. However, the higher interest rate and points apply only to the second mortgage. When this type of second mortgage is paired with a lower-interest-rate first mortgage, the combined interest rate can sometimes be lower than it would be for a single large new refinanced mortgage. It's something to consider.

TIP

I have seen some lenders include in their documentation a prohibition against later renting out property bought by a person as an owner-occupant. Check with your attorney, but I've never seen a case where this was enforced.

Is Seller Financing Really the Best Deal?

Some of the best financing for an investor (for both residential and commercial properties) actually comes from sellers. Sellers often don't care whether you intend to occupy the property or rent it out. Indeed, many simply don't ask. In addition, sometimes sellers are eager to give the buyer financing. If you find a seller in this position, you can get some surprisingly good financing deals.

Why Would a Seller Want to Finance a Buyer?

One reason a seller would want to finance a buyer is that the seller is having trouble selling the property. He or she hopes that offering financing to the buyer will lead to a quick sale.

In this situation, the seller will often overlook some credit problems that the buyer may have. After all, selling the property is foremost in the seller's mind. Thus, if you can't get an institutional loan for one reason or another, seller financing is probably your best alternative. (Interestingly, seller financing is often so good that many very successful investors buy property only when they can get seller financing.)

A second reason that sellers might want to finance a sale is that they are looking to invest the money they receive and live off the interest. This is particularly the case with retired sellers who have paid off their home, or nearly so. If they get cash for the sale of their house, they might want to avoid the risk of other investment vehicles, preferring instead to simply stick their money in a bank or a CD and collect the interest. However, a mortgage typically pays higher interest, so they may be thrilled if you give them a mortgage with an interest rate 2 or 3 percent higher than they could get at a bank.

How Do I Arrange Seller Financing?

Seller financing (sometimes also called creative financing) is arranged at the time you make your purchase offer. Instead of putting into the purchase offer a standard contingency that the sale is subject to your obtaining a new mortgage from an institutional lender, you say that the sale is subject to the seller's giving you financing. Of course, you include the desired interest rate, term, and so forth. Usually there are no "points" in seller financing. (A point is 1 percent of the loan; points are often added as a charge by institutional lenders.) In other words, you make the deal contingent upon the seller's carrying back paper. If the seller won't give it to you, there's no deal. Make the price good enough, and any seller will at least seriously consider the offer.

TIP

Keep in mind that the seller must be in a position to offer you financing. That means that the seller must either own the home free and clear or at least have a large amount of equity.

With seller financing, you'll typically get a new first mortgage for 70 to 80 percent LTV, and then the seller will give you a second mortgage for 10 to 30 percent. Thus, your total financing on the property can approach 90 to 100 percent.

Qualifying for Seller Financing

The beauty of seller financing is that there is no formal qualifying process—no application to fill out. However, most sellers will want to at least be assured that you have the wherewithal to make the mortgage payments. (Any good real estate agent will insist that you demonstrate this.) Therefore, a credit report is typically run, and sometimes income verification (where your employer confirms your employment longevity and salary) and deposit verification (where your bank confirms how much money you have on hand) are requested. However, unlike with institutional lenders, there's usually no computer scoring or other arcane techniques for evaluating your creditworthiness. (Although a savvy seller will probably request to at least see your credit score.)

It's then up to the seller to determine if you're sufficiently worthy to buy the property and to be given financing. Often it just comes down to how good an impression you make.

Not All Sellers Will Do It

In today's market, while many sellers will consider financing your purchase in order to get a sale, many others won't. They may simply find the whole process of seller financing frightening and stay away from it. Still others, as we've seen, simply don't have the equity to handle it.

When you do find an amenable seller who has enough equity, seller financing can be a wonderful option for all concerned.

Just keep in mind, however, that unlike with cash offers, you may need to make many offers on many houses before you find the right seller.

Unusual Financing Options

Shared Ownership

The first rule in real estate is that everything is negotiable, and the second rule is that creativity pays. As a result, there are all sorts of other types of financing available.

For example, I've seen family financing. A son or daughter may want to buy an investment house. He or she has the income to handle it, but not the cash for the down payment. So the parents pop for the down payment and closing costs. Then they share ownership. Typically, the son or daughter will handle the management of the property, and when it's time to sell, the family will split up the profits.

This system, of course, is not limited to families. It will work with friends or even perfect strangers. However, a word of caution: put everything in writing. People, even friends, even close relatives, often forget what was said months or years earlier. When it's time to sell, you want to have in writing exactly how the profits (or, if something goes wrong, the losses) are to be split up. Further, you want to be sure that there are solid escape clauses allowing you, or another party, to exit the deal if situations change. (For example, you could lose your job and have trouble making the payments, or your sibling, friend, or son or daughter could need to move out of the area and want to sell the property prematurely.)

All of which is to say that if you intend to use any type of shared financing, spend the bucks to have a good attorney draw up a rock-solid agreement. It won't cost that much, and it could save lots of hassle and money later on.

TIP

The tax advantages of property ownership (deduction of taxes, interest, and other expenses on investment property) can be divided among shared owners in many different ways. If you are interested in doing this, before you draw up any agreements, find out from your accountant or tax attorney exactly how to handle the tax formulas and the required paperwork.

Asset-Based Financing

Another method of financing is to borrow not on the property that you are buying, but instead on other property that you already own, such as stocks or bonds. The advantage of securing this type of financing is that you can obtain loans at very low interest rates, often through stockbrokers and banks.

Yet another financing method that experienced real estate investors sometimes use is to borrow on real estate that they already own in order to make a new purchase. For example, you may have three rental homes in which you have substantial equity. You can refinance these properties (either with individual loans or with a blanket loan covering all three) and use the funds to buy a fourth house. If you've ever played the game Monopoly, you already know the basics of how this method works.

Credit Card Financing

Some people finance their real estate purchase (at least the down payment) with cash that they borrow on their credit cards.

Is this a good way for you to buy property? No, it's not, because the interest rate on credit cards (often 20 percent or higher) will kill you in the long run. I've seen some people try this creative approach, only to eventually lose their property to foreclosure.

But I've also seen others use their credit cards on a *short-term* basis and succeed. They refinanced within months and replaced their short-term high-interest-rate credit card debt with a permanent long-term mortgage. So in the right circumstances, it can work. If you need to borrow the money just for a month or two, credit card borrowing can be an option. However, since you never know whether you'll be able to refinance in the future, it's always a risky alternative.

Retirement Borrowing

Some would-be investors are so convinced that the property they want to buy is a good deal that they'll borrow from their individual retirement account (IRA), 401(k), or other similar program. Is this a good idea?

To my way of thinking, it's not. All investments bear risk, and real estate is no exception. Using retirement money to get in should be only a last, desperate alternative. If things go wrong and you can't repay, you may not only have lost the money, but also incur penalties and additional taxes.

Stay away from this source. If you do consider it, be sure to check with your accountant and your financial planner first to learn the potential consequences.

The Bottom Line

Ultimately, if you want to buy small residential investment properties, you should be able to arrange financing one way or another. Creativity and determination often are the keys that make the difference.

Getting Agents to Work with You

When you start out in real estate investing, you're going to be at a disadvantage.

You won't know properties, you won't understand how deals are constructed, the paperwork will seem like a nightmare, and on and on.

That's why I suggest that first-time investors do not go it alone. Reading a book like this will certainly help get you up to speed on how things are done. However, for advice on your specific deals, you need professional help. In short, to help you get started, you need a real estate agent.

This is not to say that you'll always need an agent. In the first chapter, we saw how Bob and Jane benefited from the agent's (Leo's) advice. However, as they became more conversant with transactions, they needed his aid less and less.

Similarly, you would be wise to find a trusted real estate agent in your area who can lead you by the hand through your first few transactions. How to find that agent, and how much to pay him or her, is what we'll discuss in this chapter.

How Do I Find an Agent I Can Rely Upon?

Everyone who buys or sells property asks himself or herself this question at one time or another. However, the question takes on a slightly different meaning for an investor. Not only do you want an agent who is trustworthy in the sense of looking out for your interests, someone who is straightforward and honest, but you also want an agent who has experience that you can rely upon. This means someone who has been in the business a while, who has seen it all, and who can advise you not just on buying a home, but on investing as well. Where do you find such a person?

Actually, agents who fit that description do exist in almost every nook and cranny of the country. However, you may need to separate the wheat from the chaff. While the majority of agents come into the business for a few years to try their hand, especially during boom times, only a relative few stick it out for decades and make a career of selling real estate. Nevertheless, every town does have some of these career real estate people.

Traditionally, an agent with so much experience would be found in a one-person office. You could simply ask other agents which of the local agents have been around the longest, or you could call the local real estate board and see if it will tell you which brokerage firm has the greatest longevity.

However, in today's world, most successful real estate people have gone under the umbrella of a national company such as Coldwell Banker, Century 21, ReMAX, Prudential, or some other. This is particularly the case in larger metropolitan areas. In these markets, it is harder, but not impossible, to identify the type of agent you're looking for.

In real estate investing, the most important factor in your success is the agent, not the office. It's the person whom you're working directly with who will find properties for you, negotiate your deals, and look out for you.

How Do I Avoid the Wrong Agent?

First, a word about the type of agent you want to avoid. Many highly successful agents today have a very high profile in the community. They sell a lot of properties, often very high-priced ones. And they make no bones about telling everyone of their success. You can see their ads popping up on shopping carts in grocery stores, before the movies start in theaters, and in local magazines and newspapers. Typically they say something like, "Number 1 Agent in the Community!" or "Sold over One Million Dollars in Homes Last Year!" or "Top Producers." (Today many agents are working as a team, husband and wife or partners, so you'll see two faces in the ad.)

All of this means that this agent sells a lot of properties and makes a lot of money for himself or herself. But how much the agent makes shouldn't interest you.

This is not to say that you're looking for agents who don't sell. Rather, you're looking for an agent who will take the time to work with you to find just the right property. My experience is that too many of these "hot" agents just churn and burn. They hop from prospect to prospect, and if you don't buy within the first showing or two, they'll dump you and move on. After all, they have a certain volume of sales to maintain.

Indeed, one hot agent I know tells his clients as soon as he meets them not only that he is the number one agent in his area, but also that he is capable of finding the right house for them on their second trip looking. (The first trip, he says, is to let him determine just what they want.) If they don't buy, or at least make an offer, on that second trip, then they aren't really sincere. Indeed, he tells them that unless they buy then, they are wasting his time—he goes to great lengths to make the potential buyers feel guilty for not purchasing! If people don't, in fact, buy, he dumps them and moves on. There are plenty of buyers even in a down market, he says. Why waste time on those who won't act immediately?

Needless to say, he sells a lot of properties and makes a lot of money. But I can't help wondering if his clients really get what they want. Further, I wonder how well he would serve an investor who wants all sorts of additional information, such as the amount a house could rent for, how good the tenant base is in the area, how suitable the house is to be a rental, and so on.

As an investor, you don't want this type of agent. You don't want to be the victim of someone who processes real estate buyers in haste, whose eye is riveted on his or her bottom line. Rather, you want someone who is successful enough to have the time to invest in his or her clients, who is willing to take as much time as is necessary to help them, and who is determined to get for them just what they want.

What Are the Characteristics of the Right Agent?

Typically, the right agent for a beginning investor will be someone who's been in the business long enough to become financially secure—a career agent. Ideally, this person should own investment properties on his or her own so that he or she knows what it is to invest and to be a landlord. (Agents often acquire property when they don't have a buyer for it and, thus, can't get a commission—they know its value, however, so they buy it themselves.) Furthermore, this person should have enough income from his or her own investments that he or she doesn't need to churn and burn (to turn over prospects quickly in order to maintain a high volume and a high income just from sales).

That means that the right agent will probably have the following profile:

Profile of the Right Agent

1. **Middle-aged or older.** Remember, it takes a while to build up a string of properties and accumulate wealth in real estate—while there are some very excellent young agents, it's usually not done overnight.

2. **Active in real estate for a long time.** There are many private investors who have made their fortune and then turned to selling as an agent as a pastime. They rarely have the people skills to help you. You want someone who's been active in the business as an agent for a while, with five years being the minimum and ten being better. Beware of beginning agents, those who have been in business for less than five years. We all have to learn, and that's what they are doing. Only they'll be learning on you.

3. **Successful.** It's possible to be in real estate and never really make it. There are a lot of agents who are at the periphery of the field. Typically these agents have outside incomes, perhaps retirement income from another field. They dabble in property and occasionally sell a home. But they don't own much property themselves, and they really don't have a handle on how buying and selling for investment is actually done. The worst thing about these agents is that they may give you advice gleaned from their own experience, sometimes bad advice!

4. **Willing to take time with you.** The right agent will quickly realize that you're sincere about investing and will also realize that if he or she plays his or her cards right, you'll buy multiple properties through him or her over a period of many years. In short, the right agent will understand that you represent a renewable resource. Hence, the

agent will be willing to assist you, show you properties over many months, suggest courses of action, and so forth. In other words, such an agent will be interested in a long-term relationship.

5. **Honest, straightforward, and pleasant**. In addition to all of the previous qualities, you'll also want your agent to have those characteristics that every agent should have. You'll want him or her to be on your side, always. You'll want to know that you can trust what he or she says. And you'll want him or her to be able to get along with you.

TIP

The ideal agent must be assertive enough to tell you when you're wrong and to deal effectively with the other party in negotiations. Beware of agents who are too aggressive. While you may think that you'll be turning them loose on the other party, you may find they are actually putting enormous pressure on you to act quickly, and not necessarily on what you really want.

Where Do I Find the Right Agent?

We've already suggested trying to find an agent in your town who has been around awhile. However, if real estate in your area is handled predominantly by franchise or national companies, as it is in most places, then I suggest the following procedure.

Find a Local Office

Locate a large office close to the area in which you want to buy. (Remember, one of your first tasks is to identify your "farm," or the geographic area where you'll buy.) Be sure to go to that office, not to another branch of the same company.

Go into the office and ask to speak to the broker/manager. Each office is typically organized with a broker and a number of salespeople. The broker is the one who runs the show. If you go in and ask to speak to an "agent" (a generic term that can mean either a broker or a salesperson) instead of a "broker," you'll get the next person "up." This is the salesperson who's on duty that day, and he or she is often a beginner. Once you are linked to this person, you'll probably be stuck with him or her.

Other agents don't like stepping on the toes of their associates and "stealing" clients. When you get to see the broker, explain exactly what you're looking for—the most experienced agent in the office to help you get started in investing for the long term. Explain that you don't want a hotshot. You want someone who has the time to explain the business to you. (That person may turn out to be the very broker you're talking to, but it probably won't be, because brokers who run offices rarely have the time to spend with first-time investors. More likely it will be another broker who has "parked" his license there.)

TIP

Experienced brokers will often "park" their license under another broker who runs an office. This means that while they retain the ability to convert back to a broker's status at will, for the moment they are the equivalent of a salesperson. They do this to avoid the expense of operating their own office, as well as to get the benefits of being in an office with a lot of active agents and advertising. (Note that in some cases, experienced brokers may park their license in another sense: they retain their broker's license and simply rent office space from another broker.)

When you find an agent who you think is a likely candidate to be just right for you, interview him or her. Ask the following questions:

Questions to Ask an Agent

1. How long have you been active in selling real estate (not just investing on your own)? A good answer is five years or more.

2. Do you invest on your own? If so, how many properties do you have? A good answer would be 10 or more.

3. How may properties have you sold over the past year? (A good number is at least eight. That's only one every month and a half.)

4. Would you be willing to work with me (or us) over the long haul? (A wise broker will wait to answer this until he or she has had time to interview you to see just how sincere you are.)

When you've found someone you like, test your choice. Go out with this person to look at property. See what he or she suggests you do. Remember, if it turns out that you made a mistake, you can always say good-bye and continue your search.

Should I Work with One Agent Exclusively, or with Many?

This is an age-old question in real estate that I am constantly asked. Is it better to work with one agent or with several? The answer is, it depends.

When you're first starting out, I suggest that you find one good agent (as explained earlier) and stick with him or her like glue. Your loyalty to the agent will be paid off by his or her loyalty to you and the advice and help that you really need.

However, once you've become an experienced investor, you may want to work with several agents. Of course, you won't expect the kind of loyalty or attention that you'd receive if you worked with one agent exclusively. However, by then you shouldn't need it.

When you're an advanced investor, you may want to work with a stable of agents in order to have the best chance of finding a specific type of property. (With commercial, industrial, or apartment properties, sometimes agents will keep listings to themselves, so you'll need to know several to get the good deals.) You'll let these agents know exactly what you're looking for in terms of property and tell them that you're working with others. However, by then they should have confidence that you will buy through the agent who finds what you want. You'll also let them know that you'll pay a buyer's commission (explained later), if necessary, for their efforts. Making this offer will encourage the agents to continue to look for properties that you can use and to call you when they find them.

TIP

Agents value loyalty above all else. The worst insult you can give an agent is to spend hours, days, weeks, or longer with him or her looking at various properties, only to then buy through another agent. If you give an agent loyalty—work exclusively through him or her—very often the agent will reward you with superior service. However, when it comes to investment property, agents also realize that investors are looking for something special that they may not have. They realize that investors will work with several different agents in an effort to find the right property. While they won't spend a lot of dedicated time looking just for you, if what you want happens to show up, they'll be happy to tell you about it, show it to you, sell it to you, and claim their commission.

Should I Use a Buyer's Agent?

Absolutely, especially since you're an investor.

There's been a lot of talk over the last few years about "buyer's agents" versus "seller's agents," and a lot of the people doing the talking haven't really made clear what the pros and cons are. Be sure you understand the differences.

An agent must declare whom she or he works for. There are three possibilities: the seller, the buyer, or both (called a dual agency).

This has nothing to do with who pays the agent. It is perfectly acceptable for the seller to pay an agent who works for the buyer. In fact, it's done all the time.

The reason that it's important that you use a buyer's agent when you're purchasing property is that there are important issues involved. If the agent declares for you, then he or she has a fiduciary responsibility to you. This takes many interesting forms.

For example, if your buyer's agent happens to learn that the sellers are actually willing to accept $20,000 less than their asking price, your agent is duty bound to give you this information. On the other hand, if you're working with a seller's agent, that agent would be duty bound *not* to tell you, and instead to protect the interests of the seller.

Sometimes agents will declare that they are performing in a dual role, that is, that they are working for both parties. To my way of thinking, working for both parties is not acceptable. A dual agent is neither fish nor fowl. He or she can't fully represent you without hurting the seller, and vice versa. Thus, the dual agent often ends up trying to shepherd a deal through the pipeline without anyone really getting hurt. The unfortunate result for you, the buyer, is that you're not likely to get what you want: a bargain.

TIP

In almost all states, an agent must declare in writing whom he or she represents. While this can be done at any time before an offer is made, it most certainly should be done at the time you decide to fill out a purchase agreement. And the declaration should be made in writing. (Be sure you save the document. It could come in handy later on if the agent does something that's harmful to your cause.)

Some excellent agents are able to handle the dual role. But for my money, I'd go with a buyer's agent any day. Which brings up another point: who pays the buyer's agent?

Do I Have to Pay a Buyer's Agent?

If the seller pays the seller's agent, then it stands to reason that the buyer should pay the buyer's agent. However, as noted earlier, that's not how it usually works.

Typically, the seller's agent will list a property for, say, a 6 percent commission. (The commission rate is completely negotiable.) The seller's agent will then list the property with the Multiple Listing Service (MLS) or otherwise agree to "cobroker" the property with other agents. This typically means splitting the commission 50–50. Thus, the agent who finds the buyer gets half the commission. (There's no reason that can't be your buyer's agent.) And the seller's agent ends up with half. Thus the seller actually ends up paying your agent.

Sometimes, however, the seller's agent will refuse to cobroker a property. As noted, this occasionally happens with bigger investments, such as apartment buildings or commercial or industrial properties. This means that the seller's agent will want the entire commission, or at least the bigger share of it. In that case, you might, indeed, need to pay your buyer's agent a commission, or a portion of it. However, in this circumstance, hopefully, you won't mind because the deal will be big enough and generate enough profit to make the commission worth your while.

TRAP

Be wary when a buyer's agent asks you to sign an agency agreement. Be sure it does not lock you into paying a commission even if the agent can get a commission from the other side. (You don't want the agent to collect twice, once from the seller and again from you!) You also don't want to make it too easy for the agent to get the commission from you—easier than arguing with the seller's agent for it. Also, be sure that you're not liable for a commission or fee if you don't buy and that the agreement has a definite termination date. And check to see whether it allows you to work with other agents or requires you to work exclusively with one.

Can I Ask The Broker to Take Less?

This usually comes as a great surprise to newcomers to the field, and it often leads to a big mistake.

It's important to understand that there is no "set" or "fixed" or "standard" commission in real estate. That was done away with decades ago after a series of legal cases. Today, the commission is what the agent and the client agree that it is. And it can be any amount.

However, that being said, most good agents will have a minimum commission below which they will not work. They may say, for example, that as a buyer's agent, they are worth a full 3 percent (half of a 6 percent commission), and they don't want to work for less. (They will have to split that 3 percent with their office—average agents split it 50–50, but top agents get as much as 80 or 90 percent as their portion of the half commission.)

If you then badger them to cut their rate, you're asking them to work for less than they feel they are worth. Some extremely honest agents will simply refuse. They know their value.

Others may grudgingly acquiesce, but you may have poisoned your relationship with them. They will surely resent what you did, and you'll always be wondering if they are doing as good a job as they should be.

TIP

Many people feel that agents get too much money for what they do. The reason some people feel that way is that much of what a good agent does is not visible. A good buyer's agent will spend countless hours checking out property to show you, only to find that most of what he or she has looked at is just not right for you. When that agent finally shows you, say, three houses, it could be after having previewed three dozen. There's other work as well. There's the agent's expertise in negotiating with the seller, in preparing the purchase agreement, in managing the deal, and in handling the paperwork. And, of course, there's the agent's overhead for maintaining an office, car, advertising, and so on, so that he or she can be there ready to go when you need him or her. Commissions are high. But good agents do earn them.

My advice is that you do one of two things if you want to pay less. First, of course, find out how much the agent wants. Then either agree to that amount or find another agent who is willing to work for less and tells you so right up front.

How High a Fee Should I Pay an Agent When I Sell?

In the past, there were very few agents who would work for less than a 6 percent commission. (Years ago, most agents wanted 5 percent, then it went to 6 percent, and in some areas it went as high as 7 percent. On land for development it often went higher.) In fact, to help make ends meet, some offices are also trying to tack on a "transaction fee" (charged to both sellers and buyers). This extra money does not go to the agent, but instead goes to the office to cover its expenses (which are not covered because the office may be paying a top agent 80 to 90 percent of the commission he or she takes in).

Today the typical fee on residential real estate is between 4 and 6 percent. It can be higher for commercial property.

I've never met a buyer or seller who was happy about paying a transaction fee, and I expect these will fade away over time.

Should I Use a Discount Agent?

Today there are agents in almost all communities who will work on a discount basis, some with very steep discounts. That means that some selling agents will work for as little as 1 percent (instead of the typical 3 percent selling agent's commission).

Keep in mind, however, that these may not be agents like Leo, whom we met in the first chapter—they may not be the sort that you want and need when you first start investing. The reason is that these discounters may compensate for their lower commission by providing fewer services.

If you're going to use a discount broker, be sure you get in writing the exact services that the broker will perform. And be sure that the services specified are the services that you want and need.

Should I Use a Fee-for-Service Broker?

In some areas of the country, a few brokers have taken to advertising that they will perform various parts of a transaction for a set fee. When you arrange with a mechanic to work on your car, the mechanic may charge $1,000 to replace a transmission, $2,000 to overhaul an engine, and so forth. The mechanic's fees are spelled out ahead of time. You make arrangements with a fee-for-service broker in a similar fashion.

As you get more proficient in real estate, a fee-for-service agent may be all you need. After a while, you may just need to have a particular service carried out, and you should only pay for that. For example, you may need an agent to draw up the purchase agreement and conduct some negotiations with the seller. You may be willing to pay $500 or $1,000 for that. You hire the agent to do just the work you specify, based on his or her fee schedule. Then you do the rest of the work by yourself.

TIP

A fee-for-service arrangement can be particularly useful when you're buying from an FSBO seller who really doesn't know what he or she is doing. By hiring an agent to handle the contact work, you can calm the FSBO seller (who appreciates a professional third party stepping in) and sometimes save the deal.

In many parts of the country, attorneys will handle all of the paperwork in a transaction for what amounts to a nominal fee, typically under $1,500. This is the biggest bargain in legal services that you're likely to find anywhere, and you would be wise to avail yourself of it, if it's an option in your area.

Use an agent when you're just getting started. Choose him or her wisely. And you'll profit in the long run.

Eliminate Your Closing Costs

Closing costs can be deal breakers. In some cases, the closing costs can be even higher than the down payment! And in most cases, the investor has to stretch to come up with the closing costs.

Indeed, although they are seldom referred to in this way, closing costs can be the real bane of investing in real estate.

Consider this: if you buy or sell stocks or bonds, the transaction charge, even at a full-service brokerage, is likely to be only a few hundred dollars at most. (The fee can be as little as $20 or less with a discount stockbroker.) In contrast, with real estate, the closing costs are almost always thousands of dollars. For example, a seller who uses a full-service agent can expect to pay around 8 percent of the price of the home in closing costs. For the same property, the buyer's closing costs can be 2 to 4 percent. That means that the combined closing costs for the buyer and the seller amount to 10 percent or higher. On a $200,000 home, that's $20,000—a not immodest piece of change.

TIP

Interestingly, the costs of buying and selling real estate are not called "transaction costs," which is what they are, but instead are called "closing costs." I suspect that's because the latter term is less emotionally charged. A buyer or seller is less likely to complain about the costs involved in "closing the deal" than about the "costs of the transaction."

For the person who buys and sells a home every decade or so (statistically, people in the United States change homes about once every eight or nine years), the closing costs may seem like a lot of money, but not enough to make them change their habits. (When they buy and sell real estate, 85 percent of sellers and buyers still use an agent.)

On the other hand, for the investor who may buy and sell one or more properties every year, these costs can be quite onerous. If you're paying out 10 percent for the round trip, it's going to take a big bite out of your profits. Therefore, it's very important for the investor to seek ways to reduce those closing costs. We'll see just how you can do that in this chapter.

Get the Other Party to Pay Your Costs

In real estate, everything is negotiable, including the closing costs. Normally, buyers pay their share and sellers theirs (as determined by local custom). However, there's nothing to prevent your having the other party pay your closing costs.

Why would the other party be willing to do that? Actually, he or she won't. If I'm selling my house and the buyers ask me to pay their closing costs, my answer is no. What a ridiculous question; case closed.

On the other hand, if the buyers write into the purchase agreement a clause that says that their purchase is contingent on my (the seller's) paying the closing costs, now it's a different matter. Suddenly it's the case that if I want the deal, I have to pay the buyers' costs. If I don't pay their costs, then I risk losing the deal. In this case, the buyers have made the closing costs a deal point (a deal maker or breaker). And in a down market, saving the deal is often foremost on the seller's mind.

Of course, if you demand something in one area, you're likely to have to give up something in another area. If you ask the sellers to pay your closing costs, chances are that they will want you to pay a higher price. What you gain with one hand, you may lose with the other, right? Not necessarily.

Remember, since you're a buyer-investor, it's highly unlikely that you'll be going in at the full price. Instead, you'll lowball the sellers, hoping to pick up the property at a bargain price. All of which is to say that there's probably going to be a lot of negotiation before the final price is agreed upon.

When that's the case, my suggestion is that you do not bring up the matter of your closing costs. Instead, you bargain as ruggedly as you can for the price.

If the sellers ultimately agree to your original lowball figure, then forget about asking them to paying the closing costs. You're already getting the house at a bargain-basement price.

On the other hand, what's more likely is that they'll come down some and you'll come up some. Eventually, the negotiations will reach a crisis. The sellers simply won't come down any further. If you can live with their final price, then at that point agree to it *provided they pay your closing costs.*

In other words, stop arguing about price and instead turn to terms. It's positively amazing how often sellers will agree to terms if you give them their price.

For example, you may be buying a $300,000 property, and after negotiations, you're offering $240,000 and they're still insisting on $250,000. Only $10,000 separates you.

If you can live with the $250,000 price (a reduction of roughly 17 percent of the asking price—not bad), then agree to it, provided that the sellers pay your closing costs. Since these could be an additional 3 percent, that's another $7,500 thrown your way. Even better, it's in the form of cash that you would otherwise have to come up with. It's $7,500 that you don't have to take out of your pocket to make the deal.

The sales price remains $250,000. However, you get a credit toward your closing costs of $7,500.

Of course, it works both ways. When you're the seller, you can demand that the buyers pay your closing costs, or a portion of them. (Because of the commission, sellers' closing costs are usually far higher than buyers'.) They may be willing to do it to make the deal. Not so often, however, in a down market.

TRAP

Caution: Sometimes lenders will not go along with one party's paying the recurring costs of another. (Recurring costs are such things as interest, insurance, and so forth. Nonrecurring costs are such things as commissions and escrow charges.) Be sure you have an agreeable lender. Also, if the sellers pay some of your points, the question arises as to who gets to deduct or capitalize them for tax purposes. Be sure you also first check with your accountant.

Don't think that having the other party pay your closing costs is an unusual occurrence. It happens in transactions all the time. However, it will never happen unless you insist upon it. Wise investors make it a regular issue to insist that closing costs be part of the deal.

Finance the Closing Costs

A different way to avoid paying the closing costs with out-of-pocket cash is to finance them. Here, instead of the seller's footing the bill, the lender does.

Yes, it can work, but you must be careful to find a lender that is agreeable and be doubly careful to be sure that the lender is fully aware of what's happening. (You don't want an angry lender to later come back and try to either raise your interest rate or rescind your loan because some vital information was held back from it.)

To see how this works, let's assume that you're getting a 90 percent loan (putting down 10 percent of your own money). The property is priced at $200,000, so at full price, the loan amount would be $180,000, with you coming up with $20,000 down. Furthermore, let's say that there's an additional $5,000 in closing costs for you. The question is, how do you finance that $5,000?

Once again, we're going to assume that as an investor, you're not going to pay full price. Indeed, let's say that after negotiations, you can see that you and the seller will probably agree on a price of around $180,000. That means that you'll need to put down $18,000, with the lender making a new mortgage of $162,000. However, the closing costs are still $5,000.

At this point, you make this offer to the sellers: instead of a final purchase price of $180,000, you'll pay the sellers the purchase price of $185,000, or $5,000 more. And they, in turn, will give you a $5,000 credit. Is that agreeable?

Notice the difference between this and the previous deal. In that case, the sellers' credit to you for closing costs was below the final price. Here the price is higher.

This shouldn't make any difference to the sellers, since they're getting the same money either way. However, it will make a big difference to you. At a sales price of $180,000, your mortgage is $162,000. At a sales price of $185,000, the mortgage is now $166,500, or just under $5,000 more. What you've effectively done is create $5,000 more from the mortgage, which will now go to pay your closing costs—you've financed them.

There's no sleight of hand involved. All that's happened is that you're paying a slightly higher price for the property, and the seller, in exchange, is paying your closing costs. It's the same to the seller—you've just got a loan that's roughly $5,000 higher. As I said, you've financed the closing costs.

Lender Objections

A lender may object to the transaction just described. The lender may say that the true sales price was $5,000 lower, and, thus, the loan should also be lower.

To my way of thinking, this makes little sense. The loan is (or should be) based on the value of the property as determined by an appraisal. No lender worth its salt will offer a mortgage without an appraisal. And if the property is appraised at the full price (in this case, $185,000), what's the difference how the negotiations went?

In addition, the loan should be based on the loan-to-value ratio (LTV), not on the LTV plus closing costs. Thus, as long as you still put the full down payment into the property, in this case 10 percent, you should be meeting the lender's criteria for making the loan.

Nevertheless, if the purchase agreement reflects a price increase at the very end of negotiations, a lender may object, saying that the purpose is to get a higher LTV on the property than is warranted. (In all probability, the lender is simply worrying that there's some hanky-panky going on that it's not aware of, and it just doesn't want to take any chances.)

There is a way to avoid this problem. First, find a lender that doesn't object. Many do not. Then, make sure that your written offer reflects only the final purchase price. You can simply tell the seller what your final offer will be and why you want it handled the way you do. If the seller agrees, write it up that way.

Exchange a Higher Interest Rate for No Closing Costs

We have already discussed getting a bigger mortgage and rolling your closing costs into it. Yet another method is to get a mortgage with a higher interest rate. In exchange for this, the lender pays your nonrecurring closing costs. The amount of the loan remains the same; however, because your interest rate is higher, your monthly payment will be slightly higher.

These are referred to as "no closing costs loans." Check with a good mortgage broker to find out more.

Save on the Commission

The biggest single cost in a transaction is usually the broker's commission. This cost is usually paid by the seller, but if a buyer's broker was used, the buyer may have to pay some of the commission as well. If the round-trip costs for a transaction are roughly 10 percent, very often 60 percent of that amount goes to the agent. Obviously, one way to cut costs would be to sell or buy without the services of an agent.

There is nothing wrong with doing this. No one says that you must use an agent to handle a real estate transaction for you. However, as we saw in the first chapter, it's very wise to rely on a good agent's experience when you're first getting started. Only a fool would wander into an uncharted wilderness without a guide. You don't want to be that fool when you first get started investing.

On the other hand, once you've got a series of transactions under your belt, it's a different story. Now you've got the experience. And since, as an investor, you're always in the market looking for properties, you may want to handle the entire transaction yourself.

TRAP

Many investors think about getting a real estate license. This is probably not a good idea unless you actually want to become an agent. While there's nothing wrong with enrolling in a course that will teach you about real estate, the license itself can actually be a disadvantage. The reason is that lenders don't like to make their best loans to real estate agents. They sometimes suspect that agents are often making creative deals, and they worry that what's stated on the purchase agreement, which is their guiding document, may not reflect the true deal. This is particularly true when there's a commission going to one of the parties to the transaction, who also happens to be an agent. In short, agents can expect to get inferior financing. If you're going to invest, just be an investor. You don't need an agent's license.

Keep in mind, however, that while you may know that you're competent to handle a real estate transaction, the other party you're dealing with may not be as confident of this. I've often seen situations in which the seller/investor is perfectly content to sell his property as a FSBO (for sale by owner), but the buyer insists that an agent handle the transaction. Furthermore, in these situations, the buyer sometimes insists that the seller pay that agent's fee, usually half of a full commission, or 3 percent.

You may rail at the seeming unfairness of such constraints because you know what you're doing in acting on your own as a seller and you don't need an agent. But the buyer may simply say to you, "No agent, no deal." So in this situation, you can either get the agent and pay the fee or look for another buyer.

Eliminate the Points

For the buyer, the biggest cash closing costs are usually the points to get the mortgage. If you're getting a mortgage for $200,000 and you've agreed to pay 2.5 points, that's $5,000 out of your pocket. (One point equals 1 percent of the mortgage amount, so 2.5 points equals 2.5 percent of the mortgage amount.)

In the past, there wasn't much you could to reduce this expense. Today, however, with most lenders you can reduce or even eliminate the points by simply agreeing to pay a higher interest rate (as indicated previously for other closing costs). Indeed, lenders use points as a device that enables them to offer you a loan at a rate lower than the prevailing market rate.

For example, say the going interest rate is 7 percent. However, to appear competitive, the lender wants to offer a mortgage at 6.65 percent. Doing that, however, would mean that the lender would incur a loss on the loan (by lending below market). So instead, the lender collects the money up front when he or she gives the mortgage by assessing points. The lender may charge 3 points, for example.

Using a complicated calculation, it may turn out that 6.65 percent interest plus 3 points yields a 7 percent return to the lender. As far as the lender is concerned, loaning money at 7 percent straight or at 6.65 percent plus 3 points comes out exactly the same. Thus, when you try to obtain a mortgage and the lender says it's 6.65 percent plus 3 points, why not ask, "How much is it with no points?"

The lender should be able to make a quick calculation and, in this case, say 7 percent. Thus, by paying a slightly higher interest rate (and making slightly higher monthly payments), you can avoid having to pay cash up front in the form of points.

Negotiate with the Title Insurance and Escrow Companies

The last big expenses in the closing costs are the fees that go to the title insurance and escrow companies.

In the past, these fees tended to be relatively small. However, in recent years, some companies have jacked up their fees to incredible levels. Today some companies are charging two or three times what they charged only a decade ago. Therefore, if you could cut these fees, you could save hundreds, if not thousands, of dollars on a transaction. There are two ways to cut them.

The first is to simply shop around. In some states, title insurance and escrow companies compete for business, and their rates vary. (In about a third of the states, title insurance fees are set by statute and cannot be lowered; check with a good agent or call a couple of title companies to find out how this is handled in your neck of the woods.)

Where rates vary, shop around. Check out at least half a dozen companies. You may be astonished at the differences. Then, when you're making your deal, insist that the escrow and title insurance be handled through a company with a cheap rate. Once you explain, the other party to the deal should be happy to go along.

But the agent might not be. Although bundling of services (through which the agent gets a kickback) is unethical, and in some cases illegal, many agents insist that both buyers and sellers use the escrow and title insurance company of their choice, sometimes one that is affiliated with their real estate company. They often use a very convincing argument that goes something like this: "I've been involved in hundreds of deals, and the only ones that went sour were those that didn't use this company. This is the only company in which the people are reliable, and you can count on them to do the job right."

Pretty convincing, isn't it? Furthermore, it might be true. Or it might not. On the other hand, if you're cost-conscious, you may be willing to take a chance on a company whose rates are half those of the company that the agent is pushing.

Just remember that it's up to you (and the other party) to decide which escrow and title insurance company to use. The agent can suggest, but normally cannot demand.

The second way to reduce the costs is to cut a deal with a particular escrow and title insurance company, where this is allowed. After all, remember that you're an investor who's likely to bring in a lot of business. If you're there every six months to a year with another deal, particularly as the deals get more expensive, there's a lot of money to be made by the company. (Fees are usually based on the selling price—the higher it is, the greater the fees.) So tell the company that you'll deal with it exclusively. You'll bring all your purchases and sales to that company if it will give you a special rate.

Don't think this type of arrangement is something new or unusual. Title insurance and escrow companies regularly offer reduced rates to their better customers.

Even if you're just a consumer who happens to sell a house within a year after you bought it, the company may cut a deal of anywhere from 5 to 25 percent, called a "reissue" rate. If you're an investor who brings in deals on a regular basis, you may be given a regular discount.

TIP

The reason the title insurance companies say they can offer a reduced "reissue" rate to a consumer who resells a home shortly after buying it is that they don't have to conduct a long title search. They need to search the title only back to the purchase, perhaps a few months. Hence, there's less work and less cost. However, many title insurance companies conduct a search only back to the preceding transaction anyhow, so you have to wonder.

Transaction costs, strangely called "closing costs," take a big piece out of every real estate transaction. The more you can knock them down, the greater your profits are likely to be.

Tax Basics for Real Estate Investors

I f you've been involved in real estate for even a short time, you've quickly realized that investing and taxation go hand in hand. It's a sorry investor who buys or sells property without first considering the tax consequences.

One of the big pluses for real estate compared to other types of investment is the tax advantages that it enjoys. Even if you own nothing more than your own residence, you should know that you can deduct interest (up to certain limits) and property taxes from your federal income tax, and in most cases from your state income tax as well. When you own rental properties, your tax advantages can multiply.

In this chapter, we'll look at how taxes and real estate interrelate, with an eye toward how this can favor the investor. (In Chapter 4, we looked at one of the biggest tax advantages, the Section 1031 "tax-free" exchange.)

> **NOTE** What follows is *not* tax advice. It is an overview of some of the federal tax rules affecting real estate. You should not rely on this material. For tax advice, you need to consult with a tax professional such as an accountant or tax attorney.

Calculating Depreciation

If you own investment real estate, you normally can depreciate it. When you depreciate real estate, you consider a certain percentage of its "cost" (we'll talk more about cost later) each year to be a reduction in the value of the property.

Almost all business assets can be depreciated. Cars, for example, are depreciated over a life span of five years. With the straight-line method of depreciation (an equal percentage taken each year), you might take 20 percent of the cost of the car each year for five years as a loss of value. Residential real estate must be depreciated over 27.5 years. Again using a straight-line method, you would take 1/27.5 of the value each year as a loss. The value is usually the purchase price plus transaction costs less the value of the land.

Of course, the value of property usually, though not always, goes up, not down. So how can you take a loss on an asset when it's increasing in value? A helpful way to understand this is to think of it as a paper loss. Most assets deteriorate over time. Even a house will eventually fall away to dust. So instead of simply waiting until the end of its useful life span (arbitrarily decided by the government), you capitalize a portion of the loss in value each year.

> **TIP** The time span of 27.5 years is specified by the government, and it is quite arbitrary. In the past, much shorter time spans were allowed.

But, you may reasonably wonder, while the house will eventually deteriorate, the land never will. How do you depreciate land costs? The answer is, you can't. You can depreciate only the building, not the land. The only exception is land that has an asset that is depletable, such as gas or oil, and that's not usually the case here.

Is Depreciation an Expense?

Yes, it is. As you can see in the following list, it's an expense like your other rental property expenses.

Typical Rental Property Expenses

- Mortgage interest
- Taxes
- Insurance
- Water service
- Garbage service
- Maintenance and repair
- Fix-up
- Advertising
- Pool and garden services
- Depreciation

TIP

Save all your receipts! In contrast to tax accounting for the home you live in, where the only deductions are typically property taxes and mortgage interest, for a rental property you own, almost every expense is potentially deductible. You may even be able to deduct a phone, an auto, business cards, and other expenses that you incur in managing the property! Check with your accountant.

If you keep track of your rental property expenses on a monthly basis, adding them up at the end of the year to figure out your tax situation is a simple matter.

To do that, you subtract your total annual expenses from your total annual income, and the result is your profit or loss.

How Does Depreciation Contribute to Loss?

As soon as you begin to look at properties out there in the real world, you'll come to realize that there are few properties you can buy on which the income covers the actual cash expenses. When you add the paper loss of depreciation to your cash expenses, you almost always find that you have a loss for the year.

Typical Yearly Income and Expenses on a Rental House

Total annual income	$14,440 ($1,200 monthly)
Total annual cash expenses	14,000
Positive cash flow	+440
Annual depreciation	−7,500
Annual loss	−$7,060

Once depreciation is subtracted, there is almost always a loss as a result, at least on paper. In this example, an income-generating property that actually shows a positive cash flow (more money coming in than cash expenses going out) turns into a big loser as soon as depreciation is subtracted from the income.

TIP

Remember that the loss from depreciation is not an out-of-pocket expense. It's an accounting loss—it shows up on paper.

In the dim past, depreciation was a tax dodge that was used by the wealthy to reduce their sizable incomes. They would take the loss from the depreciation of their real estate (which occurred only on paper) and deduct it from their ordinary income. That reduced their ordinary income, which, of course, reduced the amount of taxes they would owe on that income.

That tax shelter was eliminated for the wealthy by the Tax Reform Act of 1986. Now it is available only if your income is less than $150,000. We'll have more to say about this shortly.

How Does Depreciation Reduce the Tax Basis of the Property?

Earlier, we said that depreciation reduces the "cost" of the building by a certain amount each year. The cost we were referring to is usually the price that the owner paid to buy the building, and that price is frequently used as a starting point for computing the tax basis. (Other costs that are considered part of the tax basis are such expenses as closing costs.)

Once the tax basis for the property is established, it is used to determine the owner's gain or loss on the property over time. If the owner sells the property after holding it for over a year, the selling price is compared to the tax basis to determine whether the owner had a *capital* gain or loss.

As we said, the tax basis for most assets, including real estate, is their cost. However, with real estate, other considerations can affect the basis. For example, you may have to pay substantial transaction fees when you buy property. Most of these fees are added to the basis. If you were to build an addition to the home, the cost of the addition would also be added to the basis.

On the other hand, the basis may be reduced. For example, depreciation reduces the basis of the property. Here's how it works:

Change in Tax Basis Due to Depreciation

Original basis (cost)	$200,000
Room added	+30,000
Depreciation	−70,000
New adjusted basis	$160,000

Notice that although the property began with a tax basis of $200,000, which was its cost, that basis went up when a room was added and, more importantly here, it went down when depreciation was calculated.

What Is the Importance of the Tax Basis?

Understanding the tax basis is important because, assuming you've held it for over a year, it (and the sales price) determines the capital gains tax you'll have to pay when you sell. Your capital gain on the property is the difference between the adjusted tax basis and the sales price.

Calculating Capital Gain

Sales price (adjusted for costs of sale such as commission)	$300,000
Adjusted tax basis	160,000
Capital gain (on which tax is due)	$140,000

Thus, returning to our example, you buy the property for $200,000; add a room for $30,000, which raises your basis; and then depreciate the property for $70,000, which lowers the basis. When you sell, both the raising and the lowering of the tax basis affect the amount of your capital gain.

TIP

It's important to keep one's eye on the doughnut and not on the hole. In general, the higher the tax basis, the lower the capital gain. Therefore, although deducting depreciation expense may make sense in the immediate term, doing so will lower the tax basis in the long term when the property is sold and will increase the amount subject to the capital gains tax, which will result in higher taxes.

All of which is to say that while depreciating real estate can produce a tax write-off, as noted earlier, when you sell, that tax loss comes back to haunt you as a capital gain.

How Were Capital Gains Treated in the Past?

In decades past, anyone, regardless of his or her income, could write off losses on real estate annually, many of which could be attributed to depreciation. What people were actually doing, however, was converting their ordinary income to capital gains income because income from capital gains *was taxed at a lower rate* than ordinary income.

Perhaps the preceding explanation went by rather fast, so let's take it again a bit slower. Let's consider just one year. In that year, the property sustained a loss of $7,000 (primarily from depreciation). That $7,000 was then deducted from the investor's ordinary income. That meant that the investor avoided paying ordinary income taxes (read "at a high tax rate") on $7,000.

Then the very next year, that property was sold, and there was a $7,000 capital gain attributable to depreciation. The investor then had to pay tax on this amount. However, because it was a capital gain rather than ordinary income, the tax rate was lower. Thus the great tax shelter benefit in real estate was that it converted ordinary income to capital gains, which were taxed at a lower rate.

TIP

Many people think of a capital gains tax as a "bad tax." However, since the maximum federal capital gains tax rate is currently 15 percent and the maximum federal ordinary income tax rate is currently 39 percent, by comparison, it's actually a "good tax."

How Are Capital Gains Treated Now?

So, can I convert my ordinary income to capital gains and reduce my tax rate? Yes—and no.

Basically, the Tax Reform Act of 1986 forbade high-income investors from taking an annual deduction for their real estate losses. However, it also provided an exception for moderate-income taxpayers.

To begin with, however, let's consider the current basic rules with regard to taking a loss from real estate as a deduction against your ordinary income. What is considered ordinary income under the existing rules?

Active Income

The tax law now discriminates among the types of income that we receive. Income from wages or as compensation for services is called *active income*. It includes commissions, consulting fees, salary, and anything similar. It's important for those involved in real estate to note that profits and losses from businesses in which you "materially participate" are included. (This does not include limited partnerships.) However, real estate activities are specifically excluded.

Passive Income

This is a bit trickier to define, but in general *passive income* means the profit or loss that we receive from a business activity in which we do not materially participate. This includes not only limited partnerships but also income from any real estate that is rented out. It's important to note that income from real estate is specifically defined as "passive."

Portfolio Income

Income from dividends, interest, royalties, and anything similar is considered *portfolio income*. We need not worry much about this here except to note that it does not include real estate income.

Under the old law, income was income and loss was loss. You could thus deduct any loss on real estate from your other income.

Under the current law, your personal income is considered "active," while your real estate loss is considered "passive." Since you can't deduct a passive loss from active income, you can't, in general, write off any real estate losses.

How Does the "Little Guy" Handle Capital Gains?

We've already said that this tax reform was aimed primarily at eliminating a big tax shelter for the wealthy. But there is an advantage in the tax reform law for the small investor. This advantage comes from an important exception to these rules. The exception provides an annual allowance up to $25,000 for write-offs for taxpayers whose ordinary income is in a moderate tax bracket. In other words, you can write off up to $25,000 in losses from real estate against your active income provided that your income is below the specified ceiling and that you meet other qualifications, such as:

Qualifications for Writing off Real Estate Losses

1. Your gross adjusted income must not exceed $150,000. If your income is below $100,000, then you qualify for up to the entire $25,000 exception. If it is between $100,000 and $150,000, you lose 50 cents of the allowance for every dollar by which your income exceeds $100,000.

   Since most small investors have an ordinary income under $150,000, the allowance applies to them. They can deduct some of their losses on real estate up to the $25,000 limitation.
2. You must actively participate in the business of renting the property.

This can be tricky—after all, what does "actively participate" really mean?

Obviously, if you own the property and are the only person directly involved in handling the rental—you advertise it, rent it, handle maintenance and cleanup, collect the rent, and so on—then you are actively participating.

However, there are gray zones. Generally, if you don't personally determine the rental terms, approve new tenants, sign for repairs, approve capital improvements, and the like, then you may not qualify.

The question always comes up, "What if I hire a management firm to handle the property for me?"

Using a management firm is an even grayer area. In general, employing a management firm is probably okay as long as you continue to participate materially (determine rental terms, approve new tenants, sign for repairs, approve capital improvements, and the like). If you are going to use a management firm, be sure to have your attorney check over the agreement you sign with the firm to ensure that it does not characterize you as not materially participating and thus prevent you from deducting any loss, if you are otherwise eligible.

Are There Any Other Kinks in the Rules?

On the surface, the allowance and the qualifications may seem straightforward. But they can be tricky. For example, here are some other considerations:

1. The income used to determine whether you qualify is your gross adjusted income. This means your income after you have taken some deductions such as retirement plan contributions (not IRAs), alimony, or moving expenses.
2. The allowance does not apply to farms. If you materially participate in the running of a farm, other rules apply. See your accountant or tax attorney.

3. Those who don't qualify for taking the deduction against their active income also cannot take the deduction against their portfolio income. (Remember that portfolio income comes from interest, dividends, royalties, and so on.)

So When I Sell, I Will Probably Owe Some Capital Gains Taxes?

Yes, assuming that you don't sell at a loss. However, as noted, the capital gains tax rate has been reduced. At the present time it's a maximum of 15 percent. Hence, even if you do have to pay, it won't be a confiscatory amount.

TRAP

You owe tax on a capital gain regardless of whether the property is an investment or your personal residence. However, if you sell at a capital loss, while you can take that loss on investment property, you can't take a deduction for that loss if it's on a personal residence! A quirk in the tax laws.

Is There Any Legal Way to Avoid a Tax on My Profits?

That, of course, is the national pastime of most Americans—figuring out how to avoid paying high taxes legally. And in the case of investment real estate, there are a few loopholes that can benefit the investor.

The first method that comes to mind is to do a 1031 tax-deferred exchange. Here the capital gain from the sale of your property is transferred (deferred) to a new property, hence there is no immediate tax to pay. A second method is to convert the property from an investment to a personal residence. You can remove the tenants (after at least a year and a day of tenancy) and move in yourself, declaring the property your principal residence. After a period of time, you may then be able to sell the home and reap the benefits of the principal-residence capital gains exclusion of up to $500,000 for a married couple filing jointly (up to $250,000 for an individual).

TIP

Keep in mind that in real estate, you owe taxes only on the gain, which is determined when you sell. No matter how high the value of your property goes, you don't pay income tax on that increase as long as you continue to own the property. (You would, of course, owe income taxes if you showed excess income over expenses on an annual basis.)

There are certain problems with this scenario, however. The first is, how long must you reside in the property to make it your personal residence? Some accountants say two years, others longer. If you previously did a Section 1031 tax-deferred exchange on the property (see Chapter 4), the holding period becomes five years (one year of tenancy after the 1031 exchange and at least two out of the remaining four years of the holding period as a principle residence). Check with your professional tax advisor.

The second has to do with all that depreciation you took while you owned the property. Some may be recaptured at a special rate. Thus, even though you may avoid paying taxes on some of your capital gain by using the personal-property exclusion (noted later), you might still owe some taxes on the recaptured depreciation losses that you took earlier.

TIP

Yet another problem here is that very often the investor is not really interested in moving into the rental property. In that case, a tax-deferred exchange (as noted above) might be better.

The Up to $500,000 Exclusion

Under the 1997 Taxpayer Relief Act, each person, regardless of his or her age, can exclude up to $250,000 of the capital gain on a principal residence. For a couple filing jointly, that multiplies to $500,000.

The exclusion can be taken only on a principal residence. It cannot be taken on investment property unless that investment property was previously converted to a principal residence. **TIP**

There are some fine-print rules involved in the exclusion that your professional tax advisor can explain to you, but the big rule to keep in mind is that in order to obtain the exclusion (assuming you didn't previously do a 1031 exchange), you must have lived in the property for two of the previous five years. That means two things. First, you've got to live in the property (not just own it) for two years before you can claim the exclusion.

Second, you can claim the exclusion only once every two years. Thus, if you own 15 rental properties, it would take you a minimum of 30 years to bail out of all of them in this fashion!

Keeping Good Records

From our discussion in this chapter, one other thing should be apparent: you need to have good records. It's very important that you keep every receipt and note every expense and piece of income.

At some point, you may have to prove to the IRS that the expenses for your investment property that you have reported were real. For example, three years earlier you had a vacancy, and you spent $115 on advertising to get a new tenant. Prove it, says the IRS. So, you reach into your bag of receipts and pull out an invoice from the local paper for $115 for advertising. Attached to it is a copy of the ad itself and your check in payment. That would be hard to dispute.

Also, keep all records of any improvements that you make to the property. Remember, improvements raise the tax basis, which will later reduce the amount of capital gains taxes that you will need to pay. (The higher the tax basis, the lower the capital gain, and consequently the lower the capital gains taxes.) If you make a capital improvement, such as putting on a new roof or adding a patio, keep those receipts, too. At the end of the year, your account-ant will be able to use them to adjust your tax basis upward.

TIP

Don't assume that just because you've spent money improving your rental, you've made a capital improvement for tax purposes. Replacing a water heater, for example, may not be a capital improvement. It may be considered a repair. Adding a tile roof where there was previously a less expensive tar roof could be a capital improvement (at least the difference in price between the tar roof and the tile roof).

Refinancing

As strange as it may seem, refinancing your property without a sale normally has no immediate tax consequences. You don't report new mortgages to the IRS. If you take cash out, however, you will have less equity to rely upon later when you do sell and must pay capital gains taxes.

Avoiding the IRS Label "Dealer in Real Estate"

In this chapter we've assumed that you will have capital gains tax to deal with when you sell your property. However, if you buy and sell many properties, particularly within a single year, the IRS may qualify you as a "dealer in real estate." What that means is that your profits are all considered to be personal income, not capital gains, and the tax can be significantly higher. Check with your accountant.

If I've conveyed nothing else to you in this chapter, I hope that I have given you the impression that buying and selling real estate goes hand in hand with tax considerations. If you're a wise investor, you'll consult with your tax professional each time before you make a new move.

The Seven Secrets of Successful Investors

What makes for success in real estate investing? What techniques are used by the big winners in the field? What are the moves that will lead to a bright future in real estate for you?

Here are seven techniques that I've observed are used by most successful investors in real estate. If you practice them regularly, you will enhance your chances of joining that winning circle.

1. Concentrate Your Efforts

Just as no one can be all things to all people, neither can an investor hope to be successful buying all kinds of properties in many different areas.

When you first decide to invest in real estate, the opportunities will seem to be unlimited. You can buy houses or condos, strip malls or apartment buildings, industrial properties or bare land.

You can choose to invest in the mountains or near the coast, in downtown areas of major cities or in the suburbs, in rural areas or in farmland. You can buy new or resale, or even build yourself. There's a type of real estate out there that will excite every interest.

What's important to understand, however, is that it's unlikely that you'll be able to invest successfully in *all* of these areas. Rather, the best way to begin is to limit your scope and then concentrate on your area of choice until you become expert in it.

In real estate, as in most other fields, knowledge is king. If you have more knowledge than others, you'll be able to discern true bargains and avoid pitfalls while others go astray. And, of course, the way to gain that knowledge is to study hard and focus your attention.

Begin with Single-Family Homes

That's why I always suggest starting with single-family owner-occupant homes. These are everywhere. They are easy to purchase and to rent out. And even if you guess wrong the first time, you're not likely to get badly hurt.

Furthermore, as you buy your second, third, and more homes, you'll get to know how the real estate market, and in particular the single-family home segment, operates. You'll become expert in evaluating these types of properties. You'll get a keen understanding of their financing. You'll be able to see those features in a home that could increase its value that its seller missed. In short, you'll develop a sense for identifying bargain property.

Of course, that doesn't mean that you're limited to single-family homes forever. It's just that this is the best way to get your feet wet. Once you've gotten some experience, it's wise to dabble in as many different types of real estate as possible.

One very successful investor I know moved his family to a mountain community and began buying and selling ranch land. Over the course of a few years, he became quite expert in the field, and he now controls many excellent ranch properties. Furthermore, agents and other new investors consult with him before they make their own purchases!

Similarly, other investors specialize in office buildings, strip malls, medical centers, industrial sites, and so on. However, these people usually didn't start there. Rather, they started small and worked into it. Most started with single-family homes.

Stick to a Single Area

I also recommend that you raise a "farm." As explained elsewhere, this is a geographical area in which you plan to buy all of your properties. It can be as small as a single neighborhood or as large as several cities. But what sets it apart is that you concentrate your efforts there and don't go far afield.

When you farm a single area, you get to know the neighborhoods intimately. You know which are on the way up, which are stagnant, and which are declining. You even know the properties block by block. For residential real estate, that means that when a potential investment property comes on the market, you don't need to waste time investigating schools and crime statistics, local government policies and homeowners' association attitudes. You already know all this. Indeed, if you're really on your toes, you'll even be aware of previous sales and be able to tell what the home is worth within a few hundred dollars.

Even further, you may have a specific location in mind. So you go door-to-door asking owners if they're interested in selling. By doing this, you can pick up homes even before they come onto the market, and sometimes get real bargains in the process.

Of course, by concentrating your efforts in one area, you also maximize the use of your time and save needless expenses. You can be close if a rental needs a faucet fixed, so you will not need to call an expensive plumber. Or if you need to find a tenant, you can put the ad in the paper, field the calls, show the property, and rent it up—instead of paying 12 to 15 percent of your rental income to a property manager. If you want to sell a home, you can easily spend time sitting in it at an "open house" when you sell it as an FSBO. (See technique 5.)

In short, concentrating your efforts in a single area is the efficient way to buy investment property.

2. Spend More Time Buying than Selling (and Be Prepared to Lose Deals)

One of the keys to successful real estate investing is to buy right. In fact, some investors feel so strongly about this that they use the motto: "You make your profits when you buy, not when you sell." By this they simply mean that the characteristics that make a property resell for a big profit are already built into the purchase. Buy the right property in the right location for the right price, and your sales success is certain. Buy wrong, and you'll spend a lot of your time trying to figure out how to dispose of the property without taking a loss.

Of course, that means that you'll need to become adroit at property analysis. It's easy to say, "Buy right," but it's quite something else to know which property is right and how much to pay for it.

One of the hardest concepts for most new investors to accept is that they'll make many offers that fall through before they get a successful deal.

TIP

It's better to lose out on buying ten properties than to buy one that's overpriced.

Suppose you find a house that you want to buy. The location is perfect. The home itself is ideally suited to be an investment. And you've determined the right price to pay, and it's only 8 percent less than the seller is asking—which is already low for the market. (If the asking price is $200,000, the offer is for $184,000.) How much sweeter and easier could a deal be?

So you make your offer, fully expecting the seller to accept. Only the seller is stubborn. She feels that the house is worth every penny she's asking, and she won't come down a dime. She won't even counteroffer!

Suddenly your perfect deal is in jeopardy. The house is right, but you can't get it for the right price. What do you do?

As in football, you punt. You move on.

The trouble is that many investors worry that they won't be able to find a better deal. They worry that maybe their calculations are wrong. They worry that while they're trying to figure out what to do, someone else will come in with a better offer.

So you go back and change your original calculations. Okay, you figure, you can easily pay 2 percent more and still come out. So you send in a new offer 2 percent higher than the last one ($190,000).

Only now the seller is emboldened. Here you're sending in a new offer without her even countering. You must want the house desperately. Why should she even think about coming down in price? So she ignores your offer. What do you do now?

Remember football? You punt and move on.

But this is the perfect house! You'll never find another that will match it. And besides, no matter what you pay, within a few years it will be worth more, and you'll make a profit. So you throw in the towel and offer the full price ($200,000), 8 percent more than you originally calculated the home is worth.

Of course you'll get the deal (assuming that the seller's ego hasn't blossomed to the point where she now wants more than the asking price!). But what kind of a deal do you have?

Certainly, over a very long period of time, you'll come out okay. (That's the beauty of real estate!) But during that time, you've lost money. You've paid 8 percent ($16,000) too much for that house. If you get into a financial bind and need to sell quickly, you'll lose money. If the property appreciates at a reasonable rate of 4 percent a year over time (counting good years and bad), it will take two good years for you to just get back to market value, not counting transaction costs. This is the sort of move that an inexperienced consumer buying one house every decade or so would make. It's not the move of a successful investor.

In short, you bought wrong, and that imperiled your profits. What's worse, you may learn the wrong thing from your efforts. You may learn that if you want to buy a house, it's not what you calculate it's worth that counts. It's what the seller is asking. You may continue to buy more properties at inflated prices, ruining your profits as you go.

The moral of our little story is that when the seller is uncooperative, think about football and punt. Remember, there are more than 65 million homes in the country, and in any given year probably up to 10 percent of them are for sale. That's a huge inventory to choose from. There's no lack of opportunity. There is, however, often a lack of fortitude. Remember, you determine what makes a deal a good one. If it's not good, you don't need to buy into it.

TIP

Many times a seller will "counter" your first offer, and then you may "counter" back. If this happens, a good thing to remember is that a counter does not have to offer a lower price. It can simply reiterate a previous price, or the price could even be higher! Don't get so involved in the countering process that you pay too much.

3. Identify the Neighborhood Loser—and Buy It

It's very rare for a good property to jump out and stare you in the face. But this often happens in the form of the neighborhood loser. This is a property that, because of some underlying factor, no one wants. And as a result, it's selling for considerably less than its neighbors.

This is a house that could be very dangerous to buy. Its detracting feature could prevent it from going up in price and could make it difficult to resell. On the other hand, if you're creative and can identify and correct the detracting feature, you can jump the property's value almost overnight.

Okay, now that I have your interest, what do I mean by a "detracting feature"?

It could be anything from purple paint to being next to a large billboard. It could be a home that's too small or too large for its neighborhood. It could have no view in an area of view homes. What makes this property easy to identify, as I noted, is that it jumps out at you. Typically, its price is far lower than its neighbors', and the problem is usually easy to see. It's a property that's crying out for attention.

A few years ago, a neighborhood loser jumped in my face. I was looking in the East Bay area of San Francisco in a town near Walnut Creek. All the homes were tract built, but they were well designed with a custom look. They were expensive, at the time going in the $800,000s. All except this one house that was listed (but not selling) for $700,000. Why, I asked myself, and I went to see it.

From the street it seemed normal enough, except that it was slightly below road level. That means that you looked down on it. This is not a desirable feature, but it is not in itself anything terrible, particularly since the drop was only a couple of feet.

However, when I went through the house and into the backyard, I immediately saw the problem. The house was literally in a hole. The homes on both sides and in back were on higher ground. That meant that the neighbors could literally look over their fences and down into the home's backyard. There was not even a semblance of privacy.

And no one wanted to buy a home where they would be under a magnifying glass. All buyers had passed on the property.

I calculated that the house was selling for at least $100,000 less than its neighbors. I offered $650,000, and the sellers accepted without countering. They were thrilled to get out. I had bought the property for $150,000 less than its comparables, not counting the poor location.

But, you may be thinking to yourself, the one thing you can't change is location.

True, you can't move the house elsewhere. But sometimes you can disguise a location. I immediately planted quick-growing shade trees along one side. When I bought them, they were about 6 feet tall. When I sold the house two and a half years later, they were 12 feet tall, and they had filled out to screen that neighbor's property.

TRAP

Beware of planting a "living fence" (trees along a property line). Some homeowners' associations and some conditions, covenants, and restrictions (CC&Rs) won't allow them over a certain height. Check first. I did.

Along the back of the property—it had a deep lot—I planted several fruit trees. After a couple of years, they not only shielded the property from the neighbor back there, but provided fruit as well—another positive.

On the final side, which was closest to the level of my property, I got the neighbor to agree to a seven-foot instead of a five-foot fence and planted bougainvillea (a plant that grows quickly and tall, clings to fences, and provides beautiful flowers). Now that side was shielded, too.

The final problem was caused by the fact that the water runoff from the neighboring properties all came through mine on its way to the street. That meant that my backyard was wet and puddled a large part of the year, and that there was standing water under the house.

A French drain (which is essentially a pipe with holes in it placed underground) collected the lot water and moved it to the street. A sump pump under the house ensured that it remained dry.

When I went to sell the house—still in the same location, still in the same "hole"—it did not look like it had any problem at all. Indeed, the backyard was a wonder of seclusion. It had beautiful flowers on one side, tall trees on another, and fruit-bearing trees in the back. It no longer was the neighborhood loser; it was a winner. And I got a good price for it, equal to that for comparable "well-located" neighborhood properties. Needless to say, the profit was very satisfying.

The moral to this story is that when a neighborhood loser jumps up and stares you in the face, put on your creative cap. Begin thinking imaginatively. Try to discover if there isn't some way you can turn that lemon into lemonade.

4. Rent Relentlessly

As an investor in real estate, you will also inevitably become a landlord. You'll own property that you will need to rent out. When you first start, you may have only one or two rentals. However, after a few years, you may have four or five, or even several dozen. With many properties, getting the rent in to cover your mortgage and other expenses is critical. Therefore, how you handle yourself as a landlord will determine to a large degree whether you'll be a success or a failure in the field.

As a landlord, you will need to rent relentlessly. By this I do *not* mean that you'll be unfair—far from it. What I mean is that you'll be all business. You won't let personal feelings cloud the issue. And, as newcomers to the landlord business quickly discover, that's much harder to do than it first appears.

I have a good friend, Joe, who's been in the investing-landlord business for nearly 35 years. Joe now owns close to 90 properties. Needless to say, he's quite wealthy. But he still handles his rentals on his own. In fact, that's his full-time job. And it's really a pleasure to watch him at it. He's fair with his tenants—I've never heard anyone complain that he wasn't. But he's all business.

For example, he has a policy of no pets in most of his properties. He feels that pets leave odors, their urine can ruin rugs, and otherwise create high wear and tear. Therefore, he does not allow them in his best properties. (He does allow them in some of his properties that he says are his "dogs.")

I'm sure that there are many readers who have pets and who, indeed, love pets. I include myself in this group. As a landlord, you will have a choice to make—to allow pets or not. Your own experience will help you determine how you want to handle this issue.

TIP

One way to help ensure that tenants who do have pets take good care of the property is to charge a large pet deposit. Most good pet owners are happy to pay this and are grateful that the landlord will accept their pets. And, in my experience, they leave the property in great shape when they move out.

Joe always asks prospective tenants if they have a pet. It's on his rental application form, and it is a question he puts to them directly. Most people answer truthfully if they do have a pet. Then he simply says that he doesn't rent the property to tenants with pets.

Where his "all-business" attitude comes in is when the prospective tenants say something like, "Well, we really like the rental, so we'll get rid of our pet."

His standard reply is, "I would never rent to people who would get rid of their pet." It's hard for a rental applicant who is a pet owner to argue with this.

When I asked him about this response, that he wouldn't rent to prospective tenants even if they agreed to get rid of their pet, he answered, "People don't get rid of their pets. When I was first in the business, I used to believe them. Then I discovered that a few weeks or months into the rental term, the pet would reappear. A person who has a pet simply won't leave it behind. They just say that they will to get the rental. So, I don't rent to them." That's Joe's acumen speaking.

By the way, it's important to understand that Joe has a pet terrier, named Charlie, that he loves. And he would never get rid of Charlie.

Joe also exhibits his business attitude when it comes time to collect the rent. If a tenant is more than a day or two late, he immediately goes to see that tenant in person. Unless it's an oversight, which it sometimes is, he insists that the rent be paid immediately.

TIP

Believe it or not, some tenants seem to simply forget to pay the rent. These tenants need to be reminded. I generally make it a point to stop by on the first of each month for tenants who sometimes forget.

I have watched Joe in situations like this, and he is all business. While tenants sometimes don't have the rent, they always have an excuse—they had a medical emergency, or their relatives needed support, or they were late getting paid for their work, or they threw a terrific party with the rent money or . . .

Joe responds, "I understand you have problems, but the rent must come first. You will always need a roof over your head, and it won't be there if you don't pay your rent. No matter what your problem, you must pay the rent first."

He explains that he's found that people always have some money available in reserve. It's just a matter of priorities. If the landlord is willing to wait, they'll put something else first. But, if the landlord insists that he or she be paid first, then the rent becomes the number one priority and gets paid—on time.

Of course, if the tenants really cannot pay, then Joe insists that they move out. But, as I said, he's fair. I've seen him give tenants $500 to help them move when they were in a really tight situation. On the other hand, I've seen him quickly go to court to get an unlawful-detainer action (eviction) when tenants wouldn't cooperate or even discuss the problem with him.

Does Joe rent relentlessly? Yes. He makes sure that he always gets his rent, on time. If he didn't, he wouldn't own as many properties as he does, or be as wealthy as he is.

Is he unfair? I've never known him to be. He provides good, clean properties at a fair rental price. He simply expects to be paid in return. If tenants have problems, he sympathizes, but he does not make their problems into his own by allowing late rent.

Will you, as a landlord, need to be as relentless as Joe?

Probably not. I find that I'm much more of a softy than he is. But then again, he owns a lot more properties than I do.

5. Sell and Buy on Your Own

When you're getting started, you definitely need all the help you can get. That includes the services of a good, experienced broker. However, once you've established yourself in real estate, you may want to consider handling deals on your own. The reason is the high transaction cost, mainly the commission to the agent.

An agent's fee is usually 5 to 6 percent for residential property (and as much as 10 percent for some investment properties). If you can handle the transaction yourself, that could be money in your pocket. And it works both when buying and when selling. When you're buying directly from the seller, you may get a price reduction for at least part (if not all) of what would otherwise be an agent's fee. When you're selling, there's no commission to pay if you don't use an agent. (Although, you may want to pay a buyer's broker's fee—typically half a full commission or around 2.5 to 3 percent, to facilitate a sale.)

However, it's important to understand that agents earn their fees. If you don't use an agent, you will have to do his or her work. That includes the following:

Things You'll Need to Do If You Don't Use an Agent

- When selling, advertise the property to find a buyer.
- When buying, scout to find a suitable property.
- Negotiate directly with the other party.
- Handle all the paperwork. (If you're not capable of this, always pay to have a professional do it.)
- Open and manage the escrow accounts.
- Arrange for financing.
- Close the transaction.

It sounds like a lot. But once you're experienced, with many deals under your belt, it will all seem doable. In fact, most experienced investors I know regularly scout out and buy properties at advantageous prices all on their own.

Here's an example: Chen works with small apartment buildings, typically four to six units. These are often built as a group in certain neighborhoods, perhaps a dozen or even 30 at a time. Once he identifies a cluster of these small apartment buildings, he goes to the county assessor's office, and by looking at the public records, he identifies the owners.

TIP The tax records for all real estate are in the public domain. If you're willing to spend the time, there's no reason why you can't find the name and address of the owners of virtually any property.

Chen then calls the owners on the phone, identifies himself as an investor in real estate, gives them the address of their property, and asks if they've considered selling. Most owners are surprised to hear that Chen knows that they own the property, and they often ask how he found them. He explains that it's not a secret.

Many of these owners will simply say no, they're not interested in selling. But almost everyone will take down Chen's name and number and promise to call when they are ready. After all, sellers figure that if they can sell directly to Chen, they can save themselves at least part of the commission!

Chen also keeps track of whom he's called, and over time he builds up a database of owners. This is his "farm." At least once a year (and sometimes every six months), he calls back or sends a note, thus keeping in contact. And sure enough, he gets calls from owners when they want to sell their small apartment buildings.

No, Chen doesn't buy from everyone who calls. Or even from every fourth one. Most sellers want too much for their properties. But every so often someone calls who wants to sell immediately, today, and is willing to offer a good price to do so. And Chen gets his good deals. When I last talked with him, he had nearly a dozen small apartment buildings and over 70 rental units, and his equity was high and growing.

Avoiding transaction costs is something that you will want to grow into as your expertise in real estate develops.

6. Hold for Market Highs

In this book, we talk a lot about buying and selling real estate. As a result, you may have gotten the impression that this is what successful investors do all the time, without regard for anything else. Nothing could be further from the truth. The savvy investor pays very close attention to the overall financial condition of both his or her area and the country, and also to the real estate market (and in particular whatever segment he or she is in).

TIP

The goal is to sell when the market is high and to buy when it is low. While this may seem obvious, determining highs and lows can be difficult.

In the residential market, savvy investors were selling properties between 2004 and 2006, during the height of the "bubble," when others were buying them. The reason was that prices had risen to historic highs, and the investors were selling for huge profits. Of course, in order to sell the properties during the "bubble," the investors had to have first purchased them. These same investors had bought these properties during the severe real estate recession of the early 1990s. At that time, prices had fallen by as much as a third of their earlier values in many areas. There were bargains galore out there. And the savvy investors picked them up, rented out the properties, and held them until times got better.

More recently, these same investors are out buying again. They're taking advantage of bargain basement prices as the real estate market bottoms.

As I said, this was an obvious move. But relatively few people actually did it. The reason was that when prices were shooting up, most people wanted to buy, hoping to resell at even higher prices. And when prices were collapsing, few wanted to buy for fear that prices would go even lower.

TRAP

The trick, of course, is knowing when we're near the bottom and when we're near the top.

The truth of the matter is that most people buy and sell at just the wrong times, spurred on by the emotion of the market. A successful real estate investor, however, will put emotion aside and buy when prices are low, sell when they are high, and hold until the right time.

All of which is to say that while it's important to be in the market, it's equally important not to churn your properties. You don't want to sell just for the sake of selling.

Being able to wait out the real estate cycle until prices move up (eventually, prices will almost certainly move up in most real estate markets because of inflation and housing shortages) is, in fact, much of the key to success in real estate. However, being able to hold means that you must have stable, rentable properties.

This gets us back to the concept of the "break-even." You will find that you can't hold on to a property with a serious negative cash flow. While you might grit your teeth and hang on to one or even two such properties, a dozen will quickly drive you to foreclosure or even bankruptcy. Therefore, to reiterate, your goal should be to buy properties for which the income comes close to matching the expenses—that is, those properties that you can sit on for years, if necessary, until prices go up and you can sell them for a profit.

However, even the best investor sometimes buys a property that turns out to be a loser. No matter what the investor tries, the property loses money each month. When that happens, my philosophy is to "dump the loser."

If you have a property that can't be sold for a profit and that is bleeding you with negative cash flow each month, sell it even if you have to take a loss. The reason: once you're rid of the loser, you'll have a better outlook, you probably will have more spendable cash, and you'll be able to move on.

Having a negative cash flow dims your perspective on real estate. You begin to think of the field as having few possibilities, and you stop looking for good deals. Indeed, I've known investors who've come to a complete halt simply because they bought one bad property. The solution is to get rid of that property and move on. You'll find that the loss, which often turns out to be smaller than you'd feared, can be made up quickly by the next, better property.

TIP

The moral is simple: sell when the market is high, and buy when the market is low . . . and dump the loser.

7. Keep Your Day Job

The best way to invest in real estate is to do it on the side and in your spare time. The reason is that you won't have much positive cash flow in the early years.

Yes, once you've been in the business for 20 years and have 10 or 20 properties that have gone up in value, with rents that have gone up similarly, you may indeed have significant cash flow. But until then, chances are that you won't. That means that you need to have a steady source of income to count on.

Married investors often keep one spouse working full-time. In addition to maintaining a steady flow of income, this also can provide job benefits such as health insurance. As a real estate entrepreneur, you're on your own in terms of all the niceties that being an employee offers. That's why remaining employed is so important.

Many single investors keep their regular job full-time and work on their real estate investing in the evenings and on weekends. In fact, if you plan on doing nothing more than spending five or ten hours a week on your real estate investments, you should thrive in the field.

On the other hand, the time you spend will probably not be at your convenience. When a good deal suddenly appears, you have to be "Johnny on the spot" to take advantage of it. That means being ready to make an offer any time—morning, afternoon, or evening.

And once you own property and become a landlord, you're going to be at the beck and call of your tenants. When there's a problem, you're the person they'll call. That could mean emergency calls at 2:00 in the morning to tell you about a leaking pipe.

Yes, it takes only a few hours a week. But those hours can be at very inconvenient times.

TIP

Not everyone should invest in real estate. When you're a landlord, it's a demanding business. You're on call 24/7. If you simply don't want to be bothered, if you want to reserve your weekends and your evenings exclusively for your own personal gratification, then do not invest in real estate. On the other hand, if you're willing to give up some personal time in the short run for long-term success, then by all means jump in.

Investing in real estate can be a no-brainer. It's a matter of simply acquiring properties one at a time until you're wealthy. You just have to make a few sacrifices, such as initially keeping your day job, to accomplish it.

Here, then, are the seven techniques that I have found successful real estate investors use:

Seven Techniques Used by Successful Investors

1. Concentrate your efforts.
2. Spend more time buying than selling (and be prepared to lose more deals than you make).
3. Identify the neighborhood loser—and buy it!
4. Rent relentlessly.
5. Buy and sell on your own.
6. Hold for market highs.
7. Keep your day job.

FAQs

The following are frequently asked real estate investment questions drawn from several sources, including robertirwin.com. If you have questions you'd like answered, or if you would like to learn about other books by Robert Irwin, check out this Web site.

Agents

Working with More than One Agent

Should I work with only one agent, or should I "play the field" and have a lot of agents looking for property for me?

A good rule to remember in real estate is that loyalty offered is loyalty returned. If you're loyal to one agent (presumably a good one!), that agent will turn over every stone looking for just the right property for you. On the other hand, if you work with lots of different agents, none of them is likely to work hard for you out of concern that even if they find a good property for you, you'll buy through someone else.

Switching Agents

Can I switch agents if mine isn't working hard?

You can and you should. If an agent doesn't call you at least once a week to let you know what he or she is doing for you, chances are that he or she isn't doing much for you. As an investment buyer, it's very easy to simply switch to another agent.

Working with a Buyer's Agent

Should I work with a buyer's agent?

When buying an investment property, you should work with an agent who declares that he or she is a buyer's agent. That means that he or she has a fiduciary obligation to represent you, not the seller. Any agent can make this kind of declaration.

Beware of buying from a seller's agent. He or she may convey any weakness you express to the seller.

I've heard you and other real estate experts say that buyers should always use their own brokers when purchasing a property. I'd like to do that, but I don't want to pay the commission. Is there any way I can use a buyer's agent without paying the commission?

This is one instance in which you can have your cake and eat it too. In most cases, the sellers, not the buyers, end up paying the buyer's agent's commission. Here's how it works. You get a buyer's agent to work for you. Since almost 90 percent of properties are listed by agents who will cobroke (split the commission with another agent), your buyer's agent should be able to work out a deal where he or she gets paid, in effect, by the seller. The seller's commission is split between the buyer's agent and the seller's agent.

Normally, it's only when the selling agent won't cobroke that you could be liable for the buyer's agent's commission. And in that situation, you can choose not to buy the home.

You should carefully check any agreement that your buyer's agent wants you to sign to be sure that you're not committed to paying a commission if it can be obtained by cobroking and that you always have the option of not buying a property. (Show the agreement to your attorney if you're not sure.) Some buyer's agents do insist that buyers pay their fee no matter what. However, I certainly wouldn't sign such an agreement in today's market.

Negotiating Commissions

What's the "fair" commission rate I should pay an agent to sell my investment single-family home? If I sell it myself, as an FSBO, and an agent brings me a buyer, do I owe him or her a commission?

It's important to remember that in real estate, there is no "set" or "fair" commission rate. Rather, everything is up for negotiation.

Furthermore, if you sell your home "by owner"—that is, as an FSBO—you normally would not expect to pay a commission at all. However, if a buyer's broker brought you a purchaser with a signed contract ready to buy, you might agree to pay that agent half a commission, which is the usual split in most areas. For example, if the average commission in your area is 6 percent (it could just as easily be 5 or 7 percent) and a buyer's broker brings you a buyer who is ready, willing, and able to purchase, then that broker would reasonably expect to get 3 percent.

In today's market, seller's agents in many parts of the country are agreeing to put a property on the MLS and in some cases do some of the paperwork involved in a transaction for anywhere from $400 to $1,500. If you're on the East Coast, a standard attorney's fee for handling your end of the transaction would be roughly the high end of that amount.

Working with Discount Brokers

When selling our property, we want to list it with a broker. But some brokers are now advertising that they will sell for a reduced commission, sometimes as low as 1 percent. Does it pay to go with a reduced-commission agent?

The question is usually one of service versus cost. You can't normally expect to get the same service from a discount broker that you can from a full-service agent (although some discount agents advertise full service). Typically, in return for the discount, you are expected to do some of the work. That may include paying for advertising, showing the house yourself, negotiating with potential buyers, and managing the escrow. In most cases, but not all, the agent will handle the documentation. It's important to remember that few things in life offer a free ride, and real estate is no exception. Someone has to do the work. If you pay full price, the agent will do the work for you. If you get a discount, you may have to do some of the work yourself.

The situation is somewhat different when it comes to finding a buyer. It's important that your home be listed with the Multiple Listing Service (MLS) so that all the other brokers in the area will have an opportunity to work on it. However, a buyer's broker's fee (as noted earlier) is typically 2–3 percent. I wouldn't list it on the MLS for any less and expect good service.

A discount broker may charge as little as 1 percent, but that's usually only for the selling agent's fee. It can cost you another 2–3 percent for the buyer's agent's fee (and the MLS listing).

Ultimately, if your property presents well and is correctly priced, it should sell either with a full-service or a discount broker. The difference is in how much of the selling work you do yourself and how long it takes to sell.

Finding a Good Agent

How do I evaluate a real estate agent? Most of them seem pretty much alike. What criteria should I use to differentiate them?

A good real estate agent is part financial advisor, part marriage counselor, and part confidant. And, of course, you expect him or her to know all about real estate. I would expect anyone who had all of those qualities to be at the least:

1. **Honest.** You want the agent to tell you when you're offering too little (or asking too much). You should be on the alert to sense if the agent is patronizing you just to get your business.

2. **Assertive.** You want the agent to be aggressive enough to get sellers (or buyers) to accept your price, yet not so demanding that he or she intimidates you into accepting a price other than what you want.

3. **Professional.** I would never list with an agent who runs down other agents or other people in the field.

4. **Experienced.** Whether an independent or from a large franchise, the agent should have five years under his or her belt, which is enough time to learn the trade. The agent should be able to provide the names and phone numbers of the buyers (or sellers) in at least five previous sales. Check the references. You'll learn a lot.

5. **Knowledgeable about investment properties.** Many agents know only how to buy and sell property for consumers. You want an agent who knows a good investment when he or she sees one.

Appraisals

Is a formal appraisal the final and best determination of value for a property?

Yes and no. It's important to understand that an appraisal is only a statement of opinion. When it's made by a professional, it's an educated opinion. But educated people often have different opinions. I've seen two different appraisers come in with appraisals as much as $50,000 apart on a $300,000 home!

If the appraisal is what you hoped it would be, go with it. But if it's far off, then consider getting a second appraisal, a second opinion. If the first and second appraisals are wildly different, you may even want to get yet another, a third opinion!

Buying the First Property

What type of property would be the best for me to start with?

I'm a first-time investor. What type of real estate should I buy?

Start with a single-family house. There usually is less risk in single-family home investments than there is with other types of real estate investments, and there are more financing options available (particularly if you intend to occupy the house for some time). Look for a newer home to avoid some of the maintenance and repair problems that exist in older homes.

Should I look for a new home or a resale? Should I buy a brand-new home or a resale when I'm just getting started?

Consider both, and go with the one that offers the best deal at the time. On occasion, brand-new homes can be purchased at bargain prices, but other times the prices are much higher than comparable prices for resales. Buy when new home prices are low, not when they are high.

New homes can be a better buy to hold (a keeper) over the long run because everything works (presumably). Keep in mind, however, that the newness of the house fixtures must be weighed against the number and types of features that may need to be finished, such as fencing, landscaping, and walkways.

Why should I buy investment property in a neighborhood with a low crime rate?

Is finding a neighborhood with a low crime rate really important for an investment property? After all, I won't be living there!

The rule is simple: never buy in a neighborhood where you're afraid to go and collect the rent at any time of the day or night. If you do, you might lose control of the property to gang or hoodlum elements. Vandalism could also be a serious problem, and it could make it difficult to find tenants.

Why should I buy investment property in a neighborhood with good schools?

Why do you insist that schools are so important? Surely tenants, who are probably transient, won't care that much.

All good parents care about their children's education, whether they are owners or tenants. Thus, being in a good school district is paramount when selecting a property, both for renting and for later resale.

While it's true that tenants tend to be more transient than owners, it's not true that they care any less about their children. And having their children in good schools is just as important to them as it is to you.

Yes, you might find a family that will move into a home in a poorly performing school district because they're only going to be there for a short time. But you don't want a property that tenants move into and out of all the time. Your cleanup and rent-up costs will be too high in that situation.

Get a property located in a good school district, and it will be both easier to rent and easier to sell.

Should I buy high-priced or low-priced property?

To some extent, the answer depends on your financial capabilities and the prevailing market conditions.

Sometimes high-priced properties are moving up in value quickly. If that's the case and you can afford them, that's where the opportunity lies. Other times, the market for high-priced properties is stagnant or even declining. In that case, stay away.

Interestingly, when the high end of the market is slow, the lower end may often be moving up quickly, and vice-versa. It's something to consider.

Comparison Shopping

What is a comparative market analysis (CMA)?

A comparative market analysis (CMA) is, as the term suggests, a comparison of comps—that is, properties comparable to the property being considered. When you conduct a CMA, you adjust for differences in features, conditions, locations, and so forth. The result tells you the market value of the property you are considering.

It's important that all the comps you use be recent. Comps that are more than six months old are suspect. Comps that are more than a year old may be useless. In areas where no comps are readily available, you may want to consult with an appraiser to get a derivative price analysis from properties that are not quite similar. (A derivative analysis "derives" the price from sales of dissimilar properties.)

You also want to account for market trends. When the market is falling, discount the CMA an appropriate amount. (If it's falling 6 percent a year, discount it by 3 percent if you plan to flip it within six months.) If the market is rising, add an appropriate amount to the CMA.

Condominium Units versus Single-Family Homes

Should I consider buying a condo as an investment property? I can get one for half the price of a single-family home in my area.

Condos are not simply cheaper single-family homes. They are a different type of lifestyle.

In general, condos do not make good rentals. The other owners, through their homeowners' association, often get in the way of acquiring tenants. You may not, for example, be able to put up a sign in front of the development. Or you may be restricted as to the term over which you can rent out the property to tenants.

If you do decide to go with a condo investment, try to find one in a development where there are few other rentals. Having more than 25 percent rentals in a complex may make it difficult to get financing, both when you buy and when you want to resell. It may also drag down the appeal of the development, making it more difficult to get good tenants.

Conversions from Owner-Occupant to Rental

If I buy a home as an owner-occupant, how long must I live in the property before I can convert it to a rental?

The lender usually wants to be sure that you "intend" to live in the property. Intent is normally demonstrated by moving in and living there. (Of course, you may be prevented from moving in by forces beyond your control, such as a job change or an illness.)

I don't know of a hard-and-fast rule that specifies how long you must live in the property before you can safely convert it to a rental. Lenders to whom I've spoken, however, suggest that a year is probably a reasonable time. Be sure you check with your attorney before making the decision.

Conversion from Rental to Owner-Occupant

How long do I need to rent out a home after a 1031 tax-deferred exchange before I can convert it to my personal residence, resell it, and claim the up to $250,000 per single person, up to $500,000 for married couple filing jointly capital gains exclusion?

For tax advice, check with a professional in the field. The following should not be considered advice. Tax rules change constantly, and you should not rely on this material.

Many investors who have significant capital gains would like to convert a rental to a personal residence and then claim the big exclusion to avoid paying taxes on that gain. There are, however, three steps to the process. The first is typically a 1031 tax-deferred exchange in which the rental is traded for a like-kind rental home that would be suitable for a personal residence.

The second step is to continue renting out the property for a period of time so that the government can't challenge the 1031 tax-deferred exchange. This is a gray area, and there is no defined time for which you must rent out the property. Accountants with whom I've spoken, however, have suggested that a year should be enough. Check with your own accountant on this.

Once you move into the house and convert it to a personal residence, however, there's nothing gray about it at all. You must live in the property for five years after doing a 1031 exchange in order to claim the exemption. Only then can you sell and hope to get the up-to-$250,000 ($500,000 for married couples) exclusion. But, as I said, we're talking about complex tax maneuvering. You should check with your own accountant or tax attorney before taking any action. (See also Chapter 13.)

Deposits Accompanying Purchase and Sale Agreements

How long do I have to get my deposit out of a purchase agreement on an investment property? Can I buy contingent on a physical inspection, then, if I don't like the inspection, back out and still get my deposit back? What if I discover something about the property at the final walk-through? Can I cancel the deal and get my deposit back then?

Most purchase offers boldly state that you are signing a legally binding agreement. If you don't want to buy the house, don't make the offer or agree to the counteroffer. If you do sign, be resigned to the fact that you have bought it. Your deposit is part of your guarantee to purchase.

Having said that, it's important to keep in mind that many states leave "outs" for buyers. For example, California allows three days for the buyer to examine a seller's statement of disclosures about the property. If you don't like what the seller discloses within three days, you're often able to get out of the deal during that time frame.

Also, a well-written purchase contract will offer the buyer the opportunity to get and approve a professional home inspection report. If you don't like what the report says, disapprove it, and you're usually out. (Some contracts specify that there must be significant problems found for the buyer to get out of the deal.)

Even the federal government allows 10 days' opportunity to have a lead inspection of the property. If you find lead and you don't approve—again, you're probably out of the deal.

This does not, however, usually apply to the final walk-through. Here the point is to provide the buyer the opportunity to see that the house is the same as it was when the offer was made a month or so earlier. Unless there is some new damage or problem found, it's unlikely that you can use anything you discover at this time as an out. Indeed, most purchase agreements specifically state that the final walk-through is not to be used as a tool for getting out of the deal.

All of this is moot, however, if the seller decides to challenge it. You should check with a good real estate agent or attorney before trying any such ploy. Remember, it's called a good-faith deposit, meaning that it is your proof that you intend to go through with the deal. Don't offer it unless you plan to follow through.

Disclosures on the Condition of the Property

When buying a house "as is," is it necessary to get a separate professional inspection, or can I rely on the seller's disclosures?

A professional inspection should be the rule for every investor who's not capable of conducting this inspection himself or herself (which means about 99 percent of investors!). This is especially true when the seller offers the property "as is." Normally, sellers don't sell that way unless there's something seriously wrong with the house; offering to sell as is puts most buyers off and often results in a lower sales price That's why most sellers don't use it. On the other hand, it's a real come-on to investors.

It's important to understand that just because a seller offers a property "as is" doesn't mean that he or she does not have to disclose defects. Indeed, disclosure is doubly important here. However, some sellers conveniently forget a few "minor" troubles with the property. While this might be grounds for legal action after the sale, it's always better to get this problem out in the open and dealt with before the deal closes. And a good physical inspection is the right way to attack it.

Financing

Preapprovals

Should I get preapproved if I'm looking to buy a home as an investor?

Yes. And doing so is even more important if you plan to live in your first investment home.

Preapproval is a process whereby a lender looks at your financials and tells you how big a mortgage you can get and, as a result, how big a property you can buy. If you are buying as an owner-occupant, this step is necessary in order to let you know what you can afford as well as to prove to the seller that you have the ability to conclude the purchase.

If you are buying as an investor, this step is necessary in order to let you know what type of financing is available to you, how much cash you need to put down, and how expensive a property you can afford. The preapproval process for investors who do not intend to live in the property they buy may not be as heavily weighted toward an underwriter's approval and credit scoring because the LTV is typically lower and may not involve a conforming loan (one purchased by Fannie Mae or Freddie Mac on the secondary market), but it is, nonetheless, a quick way to determine what a lender will do for you.

Points

What are points?

One point is equal to 1 percent of a mortgage. Two points are 2 percent, and so on. Points are tacked onto your closing costs to increase the yield of the mortgage to the lender. You can sometimes reduce the points (sometimes to zero!) by increasing the interest rate you pay. This is a great way to save money if you're short of cash. Check with your lender as well as Chapter 12.

Creative Financing

I've heard the term creative financing. What does it mean?

It means any financing that's out of the ordinary course of getting an institutional loan from a lender, such as a bank. For practical purposes, it simply means financing that's handled by the seller.

Private Mortgage Insurance (PMI)

Is there any way to avoid the additional cost of private mortgage insurance (PMI) when buying a home with only a 10 percent down payment?

Any time you get a mortgage for more than 80 percent, the lender is going to want private mortgage insurance. There is, however, a way to get around it, even when you can afford to put only 10 percent (or less) down: get an 80 percent mortgage and then a second 10 percent mortgage (putting the remaining 10 percent as cash down). You can expect the second mortgage to have a slightly higher interest rate than the first, but the combined rate of the two mortgages should be lower than the combined rate of a big 90 percent mortgage plus PMI. First and second loans are available from institutional lenders. Second mortgages can sometimes be obtained from sellers.

How do I get the PMI removed on a house I bought to live in a year ago and now want to convert to a rental?

Removing the PMI portion of the loan is of great interest to low-down-payment borrowers, as it can shave as much as a hundred dollars or more off the monthly payment. To help borrowers who wish to pursue this course of action, a federal law was passed to require lenders of recent mortgages to remove the PMI when the equity increases to 22 percent of the value. However, in order to get it removed when home prices go up, you must contact your lender and arrange for a new appraisal. Most lenders have a procedure for doing this. Some lenders, however, are a bit slow on the uptake, and it may take several calls and/or letters to get action. Just be sure your equity has, in fact, increased sufficiently, or else you'll just be spinning your wheels.

An alternative may be to refinance to a new mortgage. As long as the loan-to-value ratio (LTV) is 80 percent or less, no PMI is required. No-closing-cost refinancing is widely available, and you should have a good mortgage broker evaluate your current loan to see if going this route makes financial sense for you.

Adjustable-Rate versus Fixed-Rate Mortgages

Where can I find the lowest-cost mortgage? Should I pursue a variable-interest-rate mortgage or a fixed-interest-rate mortgage?

The rule is that you get a fixed-rate mortgage when rates are low to lock them in. You get a variable-rate mortgage when interest rates are high, so that your interest rate will drop as the market comes down. In a high-interest-rate market, it can sometimes be advisable to try to find a two-step, in which, for a small fee, you can convert a variable-rate mortgage to a fixed-rate mortgage after a set period of time, say, two to three years. By then interest rates may be dropping, and you will want to lock in the lower rate.

Beware of adjustable rate mortgages with low initial "teaser" rates that then reset to a higher rate and payment within a few years. If the market changes and you can't refinance or get a better loan (or resell) when the original mortgage resets, your payment could shoot up and you could lose the property. This in large part is what caused the "foreclosure bust" of 2007 and 2008.

There are many Web sites through which you can access mortgage brokers and dozens of different financial institutions. Try eloan.com, quickenloans.com, and lendingtree.com. If you don't want to use the Web, consider a mortgage broker in your area. Get a recommendation from a real estate agent. Most good mortgage brokers these days work with dozens of financial institutions.

Fixer-Uppers

Should my first investment property be a fixer-upper?

No. Go with a home that's in good condition. You'll have enough first-timer problems to deal with without having to worry about renovating the property before you can rent it out.

Fixer-uppers (handyman specials) are great for the experienced investor, someone who knows the ins and outs of real estate transactions and who is handy at fixing things to boot. Extra profits can be made here.

When you're just starting, however, you increase your risks by taking on too much all at once. Stick with just learning to buy and sell. Leave the fixing up for later.

How do I evaluate a run-down property? How do I know if a property will make a good fixer-upper?

It's not hard. But, then again, it's also not easy.

Run-down property can have anything from minor cosmetic blemishes to severe damage. The way to evaluate a property is to make a very accurate calculation of how much it will cost to put the property into tip-top shape. Then find out how much it should sell for in that final shape and subtract the costs of fixing it up. Also subtract your own profit and transaction costs. If you can get the house for the final, low price, it's probably a good deal.

Flipping

Does flipping really work?

Yes, it certainly does! Flipping often means that you sell a property as soon as (or even before!) you take title. It's a way to make big profits very quickly in real estate.

Be aware, however, that good flippable properties are few and far between. This is particularly the case in a slow market.

Check to see if the market is right for flipping properties. You can ask local agents, or try my test: check with developers of new homes. If there are long lines of people waiting to buy homes, it indicates a market shortage and strong demand—the right fodder for flipping. If developers are wringing their hands and cutting prices because there are no buyers, flipping is probably not an option.

Foreclosures

Where can I find foreclosed properties?

There are many sources. The best source is the Internet. Check in sites such as www.foreclosure.com or www.realtytrac.com. They usually list preforeclosures, auctions, and lender-owned properties. Additionally, sometimes people in preforeclosure will advertise for buyers in the local newspaper.

Lenders typically list REOs (properties they've taken back through foreclosure) with real estate agents. These agents then usually advertise these properties in the newspaper.

Inspections

Does every investment property I buy need to be inspected?

I'm buying a new home as an eventual investment. Do I need a home inspection?

There's a common misconception among new-home buyers that they don't need a home inspection. Every home, new or old, should be inspected prior to purchase. Of course, you're more likely to find problems in older homes. But new homes have their share as well. You need a good home inspector who will check out the concrete foundation, the walls and roof, the electrical and plumbing systems, and all the other home parts for you. Just because it's brand new doesn't mean it was built right.

How do I find a reliable inspector? Are there any organizations that regulate home inspectors?

Not all states regulate home inspectors. However, many inspectors belong to one of the national trade organizations, and many belong to local trade groups as well. Most of these offer minimum "standards of practice" that inspectors are expected to follow. Check out www.nachi.com (National Association of Certified Home Inspectors) or www.ashi.com (American Society of Home Inspectors).

Who should do repairs?

If the sellers disclose, or the physical inspection reveals, damage that needs to be repaired, is it all right to have the seller do it? Or should I insist that professionals do the job?

When you are having work done to a roof or anything else in a home as part of a purchase, it's always important to specify in the sales contract that the work must be done in a competent manner in accordance with accepted professional standards. It's a good idea to even specify that it must be done by a professional, not by the homeowner. For work that was done recently (and sometimes not so recently), it's also a good idea to request copies of the building permit and the contractor's agreement.

Too often, sellers will try to do repair or deferred maintenance work themselves and will botch the job. The result is that it looks bad or simply does not work (a roof may continue to leak, for example). It's better to insist that it be done professionally and not have to worry about it.

Investing

How much money do I need to get started? Do I need a lot of money to get started investing in real estate?

No. That's a common misconception, probably caused by the fact that property costs so much. Today there's still excellent financing that can help you get into your first home. Indeed, if you have a solid job with a good income and good credit, you may not even need a dime to get started! (See Chapter 10 on financing.)

Should I live off my investment income? Can I make a living investing in real estate?

Yes, of course you can. But probably not right away. Never mind what the so-called gurus tell you. When you're getting started as an investor in property, chances are you'll have very little positive cash flow coming to you. Indeed, for a few years you may need to feed those properties (put in money each month just to keep them going)!

Real estate investing is a long-term process. After you've been doing it for a number of years, your cash flow should increase to the point where you can live off it. However, until then, it's best to do it as a part-time business, a few hours a week. In other words, when you're getting started, keep your day job!

Land

Using a Buyer's Broker in Land Purchases

Should I use a buyer's broker when buying rural or bare land?

A buyer's broker will prove invaluable to you if you're inexperienced in land purchases. Undoubtedly the broker will insist that the seller provide a land survey to prove exactly where the land you are buying is located, as well as to determine if there are any encroachments. He or she will also check with utility companies to confirm that the hookups are coming to your lot. If the broker is familiar with the area and knows of geological problems, a soils report will be in order. This, of course, is in addition to the usual title report. Finally, the buyer's broker may be able to negotiate a better price or terms for you.

Of course, there is the cost. But very often a buyer's broker will be able to negotiate with the seller to be paid half the selling commission, in which case your costs would be nothing. (See the section of this chapter on agents.)

Purchasing Bare Land

Bare land and farmland are often advertised at what seem to be very low prices. Are the prices indeed low, and should I take advantage of such apparent bargains?

If I had a chance to purchase a property for $300,000 for which someone else was willing to pay $600,000, I don't think I'd let much stand in the way of my purchase! On the other hand, I learned long ago that when something sounds too good to be true, it usually is.

When land is advertised at a super low price, there is often a problem with it. It might be that there's not enough water, or too much. It could be that the soil is too rocky or too soft for building. It might be that there is simply no power available in the area. Or it could be something else.

My suggestion is that you first consult with a good real estate agent located in the area who knows the type of property and who can tell you what problems are likely to exist. Also, have the agent give you both a written market comparison analysis and a thorough appraisal before you buy. This will tell you the property's true value. It will let you know whether you've really got a great deal, or whether you're the subject of a scam.

If, indeed, you can buy land for significantly less than market value, consider flipping. All you need to do is tie it up and then resell it. You can use a contract in which you have the right to assign the purchase. You can then assign it to another buyer right out of escrow, pocketing your profit. Alternatively, you can try for an option on the property and then sell the option rights to the new buyer, again pocketing your profit. In short, any good real estate attorney should be able to help you make your profit quickly. (Also see Chapter 5.)

Location

Where should I buy my investment rental property?

Always buy it as close to home as possible. Hopefully, you'll never own a property that is more than half an hour's drive away. That way you can handle rent-up, respond to tenants' complaints, collect rent, deal with late payers, and do much of the maintenance and repairs yourself. Long distance is no way to own rental real estate.

Profits

Cashing Out

How do I get my profits out of my investment property?

There are many ways. If you've owned a property for a number of years, chances are that your rents have increased to the point where they exceed your expenses. Thus, each month your property pays you.

Of course, you can always sell a property and get your equity out in either cash or paper (a mortgage with you as the lender).

Or you can refinance to get cash out.

Keep in mind, however, that property is not liquid in the financial sense. It's not like a checking or savings account from which you can simply demand the money and it's there. That means that while you can get your money out, it can take time to do it—weeks or months (or, in a very bad market, sometimes years). On the other side of the coin, however, the profits are usually far and away superior to anything you can get in a demand money account.

Increasing Profits

How do I increase the profits on an investment property?

Your property usually will go up in value over time all on its own because of inflation and the general shortage of most types of real estate in the country (particularly housing). However, you can increase the value of commercial real estate (apartment houses, industrial properties, office buildings, and so forth) by increasing the rents. The more rent the property commands, the more it's worth, and the higher the price you can sell it for.

Real Estate Owned Properties (REOs)

What is an REO?

A real estate owned property (REO) is one that a lender, such as a bank, has taken back through foreclosure. The lender is then the owner and typically is anxious to sell. You can often negotiate a good deal with a lender on an REO if you can demonstrate that you have the cash and credit to handle the deal. However, today most REOs are listed with agents, so plan on going through them. (Also check into Chapter 3.)

Rental Properties

Repairs

How long can I put off a tenant who calls in the middle of the night to say that a water heater is broken or a faucet is leaking?

If it's a water heater, you'd better go out right away, even if it is the middle of the night. A leaking water heater can potentially ruin the flooring in a home if it leaks inside. You'll at least want to get out there to turn off the water (or tell the tenant how to do it). A leaky faucet can wait until morning or the weekend.

It's important, however, that you fix all problems with the property as soon as possible. Landlords who refuse (or delay unnecessarily) to remedy problems that affect the habitability of a property may find that the tenants have fixed the problem by calling in an expensive plumber, electrician, or whatever, then deducting the costs from their rent! Some states give tenants the right to do this, and you just might be up the creek.

Raising Rents

How quickly can I raise rents after I buy a property?

It all depends on the market. If there's a shortage of rental housing and the market goes up quickly, you can raise your rents quickly. Keep in mind, however, that if you raise rents too quickly, your tenants could move out. Be sure to factor in the costs of cleanup and rerenting.

Keep in mind that how much you can charge for rent has nothing whatsoever to do with how much you want or how much your expenses are. It's strictly market-driven.

Deposits

Why can't I just keep the cleaning-security deposit? After all, most tenants leave the place in such a mess that some cleanup work is always required.

A cleaning-security deposit must be returned to a tenant who leaves the property in the same condition as it was found, "reasonable wear and tear excepted." That means that there is always going to be some wear and tear on the property, including wear of carpets, fading of paint, and so on. These are to be expected no matter who lives in the property, and they are your problem, not the tenants'. However, you can reasonably deduct the cost of repairing deep scratches in the walls or stains on the carpets, for example. What you can and can't subtract is a highly technical matter. Check into Chapter 9 for more details.

Most states require that you give tenants an accounting of the security-cleaning deposit within 14 to 30 days after they move out, explaining how every dime not returned to them was spent.

Selling

Slow-Selling Properties

I can't sell my investment house. I've fixed it up, even put in new carpeting and completely repainted it inside and out. What could be the problem?

Sad to say, the most common reason for a property not selling is that it's simply priced too high for the current market. If it doesn't sell, immediately get a good comparative market analysis (CMA). Any agent can perform one for you, or you can get it done via the Internet. You need to find out exactly what comparable houses are selling for. If the price for yours is higher, that would explain why it's not selling. (Don't forget to subtract a discount if the market is falling.)

Lease Options

Should an investor seriously consider using a lease option to sell a piece of property?

The lease option has been around for many years, and it is a legitimate method of selling property; however, it's more commonly used in a down market. It involves leasing the property to a hopeful buyer along with an option to buy at a set date and usually at a set price. A portion of each month's rent is applied toward a down payment. At the termination of the lease, when, hopefully, the down payment has been reached, the buyer gets a mortgage, and the sale is completed.

With a lease option, you can have all the problems inherent in renting, including maintenance and the possibility of having to evict the tenant for nonpayment of rent. These risks, however, can be minimized by getting a hefty security deposit and by carefully screening the applicant, making sure that your tenant has a previously successful rental history.

The cause of most problems with lease-option arrangements is that either the amount of the rent that goes toward the down payment is not sufficient or the tenant-buyer cannot qualify for a mortgage to complete the purchase when the term of the lease expires. One solution is to get the person preapproved for the eventual financing before renting out the property. In that way, you have some assurance that the eventual buyer can qualify for financing; you will also learn just how big a down payment will be needed, and you can adjust the rent accordingly. The problems with this approach are that interest rates fluctuate and people's credit standing changes. The buyer who qualifies today may not be able to do so tomorrow.

Note that some states, such as Texas, severely restrict an owner's ability to use the lease option. Check with a local attorney in your area for any restrictions your state may impose on you. Some experts swear by the lease-option approach. Over the years, however, I have found it to be bothersome.

Taxes

For tax advice, check with a professional in the field. The following should not be considered advice. Tax rules change constantly, and you should not rely on this material.

Deductions

When I buy a property, I understand that I can deduct my mortgage interest and my taxes. Is that a straight one-to-one deduction (a dollar off my taxes for each dollar I spend on interest and taxes)?

No. Confusing a deduction with a credit is a common mistake for first-time investors. What you've described is a credit. What you get is a deduction. That means that on a principal residence, you may be able to offset your income (not your tax liability) by your expenses for mortgage interest and taxes. Lower adjusted income, of course, could result in lower taxes.

On an investment property, you subtract all of your expenses from your rental income. If you have a loss, you might (or might not) be able to deduct it from your personal income. Check into Chapter 13 for an overview of the tax rules.

I've heard that some investors can't deduct their losses in real estate from their personal income. Is that correct? Why?

It all has to do with the active-passive rules passed by Congress more than a decade ago. Very briefly, if your income is above $150,000, then you probably can't deduct any losses incurred on your investment real estate from your personal income in the year they occur. If you earn between $100,000 and $150,000, you may be able to deduct 50 cents in losses for each dollar. If your income is under $100,000, you may be able to deduct up to $25,000 of your loss.

This is a very complex subject, and you shouldn't rely on the very brief explanation given here. Check with your tax attorney or accountant to see how you fare.

Timeshares

Do timeshares make good investments?

No, they usually don't. The truth is that there is a very small resale market for timeshares. When you want to sell, chances are you will find that there are few to no buyers, at least not at the price you originally paid.

On the other hand, I know many people who own and enjoy going to their timeshare each year and who successfully trade for other locations, some in expensive foreign cities. With the price of hotel rooms going up everywhere, timeshares are making more vacation sense than ever before.

Nevertheless, I don't know any timeshare owners who have sold their property for a profit or who have even reached the break-even point (although I'm sure there must be someone out there who has done so). In short, a timeshare doesn't really meet the basic requirement of an investment—that it produce a profit. If you like it, buy it because you'll enjoy it, not because you'll make money on it.

Transaction Costs

I recently bought my first investment property, and just as I was going to sign the loan documents, the agent told me that there was an additional "transaction cost." Is this legitimate? Do I have to pay it?

Some real estate offices have taken to charging transaction fees to help offset their costs of doing business. It's a way of charging more without actually raising the commission rate. (Sort of like the garbage fees that some lenders charge to increase their yield on a mortgage without increasing the interest rate.)

As a buyer, unless you've previously agreed in writing to pay a transaction cost, you probably don't have to pay it. The question becomes, will the agent dump the deal because you refuse to pay a few hundred dollars? In today's market, I doubt many agents will.

On the other hand, when it comes time to resell, read the listing agreement carefully from beginning to end. It's a legally binding document. If it contains a clause specifying a transaction fee, you probably would be bound to pay it.

Index

need for, 254–255
VA repos, 84–85
Inspectors, finding reliable, 254
Instincts, trusting your, 155–156
Insurance
    as expense, 203
    as fixed expenses, 135
    private mortgage insurance
        (PMI), 137–138, 250–251
    title insurance, 76, 197–199
Interest
    as expense, 203
    interest rates, 195
    points, 36, 250
    as tax deduction, 262–263
Internet and Web sites
    advantages of working, 148
    APOD annual property operating
        data (APOD) sheet, 120
    author's site, 129
    capital gains calculator, 92
    finding inspectors, 254
    foreclosures on, 20, 22–23
    for-sale-by-owner homes
        (FSBOs), 148–149
    HomeSteps program, 87
    HUD, 81, 154
    landlord's associations, 157
    mortgage loans, 252
    real estate listings, 45
    rental applications, 154–156
    Section 1031 exchange, 92, 98
    200 percent rule, 96
    VA repos, 84
Interviews with agents, 181
Investing in real estate (See specific
    topics)
Investors, successful (See Secrets of
    successful investors)

J
Job, investing as, 58–59, 233–235,
    255–256

K
Knowledgeable about investment
    property, agent as, 176–177,
    241

L
Land
    buyer's brokers, 256
    buying for investment, 256–257
    depreciation, 202–203
    development of, 118, 126
Landlords
    agents as, 178
    associations of, 157
    making repairs, 259–260
    "on call 24/7," 234
    recommendations from, 155
    (See also Residential rental
        property; Tenants)
Lawn services as expense, 203
Lawyers (See Attorneys)
Lease evaluation for office building,
    49–50
Lease option to sell, 261–262
Lenders and banks
    closing costs, 192–194
    demonstrating cash flow, 122–123
    financing deals with agents, 196
    foreclosures, 28–29
    preapproval, 20, 74, 249
    recurring costs, 100
    working with, 28–32, 194
    (See also REO [lender-owned]
        property)
Length of lease, 50

About the Author

Robert Irwin (Westlake Village, CA) is one of America's most respected experts in all areas of real estate and the author of more than 20 books, including the bestsellers in the McGraw-Hill Tips and Traps series.